The
Great Big
Book of
Bedtime
Stories
and Rhyme

QED Publishing

Copyright © QED Publishing, 2007

First published in the UK by
QED Publishing
A Quarto Group Company
226 City Road
London EC1V 2TT
www.qed-publishing.co.uk

ISBN 978-1-84538-883-6

Publisher: Steve Evans
Creative Director: Zeta Davies
Senior Editor: Hannah Ray

Printed and bound in China

The Great Big Book of Bedtime Stories and Rhyme

Contents

When I'm a Grown-up

Anne Faundez

Illustrated by Katherine Lucas

When I'm a grown-up,
Who will I be?

A bird in the air,

Or a fish in the sea?

11

When I'm a grown-up,
What will I do?

12

Fly a spaceship to Mars,
Or work in a zoo?

13

When I'm a grown-up,
Will I be tall?

Huge like a hippo,

Or round like a ball?

When I'm a grown-up,

Who will live with me?

A frog or a dog?

Or a hoppity flea?

21

When I'm a grown-up,
Will I travel by car?

24

Ride on a rhino,

Or swing from a star?

25

When I'm a grown-up,
I really don't mind
Who I will be...

As long as

I'm

ME!

Sing a Song of Sixpence

Compiled by Anne Faundez
Illustrated by Simone Abel

Sing a Song of Sixpence

Sing a song of sixpence,
A pocket full of rye,
Four and twenty blackbirds
Baked in a pie.

When the pie was opened,
The birds began to sing,
Wasn't that a dainty dish
To set before the king?

The king was in his counting house,
Counting out his money,
The queen was in the parlour,
Eating bread and honey.

The maid was in the garden,
Hanging out the clothes,
When down came a blackbird
And pecked off her nose.

Little Jack Horner

Little Jack Horner sat in a corner
Eating his Christmas pie.
He put in his thumb and pulled out a plum,
And said what a good boy am I!

Little Miss Muffet

Little Miss Muffet
Sat on a tuffet,
Eating her curds and whey.
Along came a spider
Who sat down beside her,
And frightened Miss Muffet away.

One, Two, Three, Four, Five

One, two, three, four, five,
Once I caught a fish alive.
Six, seven, eight, nine, ten,
Then I let it go again.

Why did you let it go?
Because it bit my finger so.
Which finger did it bite?
This little finger on the right.

Two Little Dicky Birds

Two little dicky birds
Sitting on a wall,
One named Peter,
One named Paul.

Fly away, Peter!
Fly away, Paul!
Come back, Peter!
Come back, Paul!

Old King Cole

Old King Cole
Was a merry old soul,
And a merry old soul was he.
He called for his pipe and
He called for his bowl,
And he called for his fiddlers three.

Cock a Doodle Doo!

Cock a doodle doo!
My dame has lost her shoe,
My master's lost his fiddling stick,
And doesn't know what to do.

39

Hush, Little Baby

Hush, little baby, don't say a word,
Mama's going to buy you a mocking-bird.

And if that mocking-bird don't sing,
Mama's going to buy you a diamond ring.

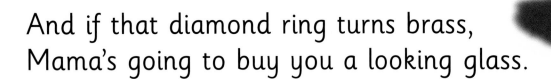

And if that diamond ring turns brass,
Mama's going to buy you a looking glass.

And if that looking glass gets broke,
Mama's going to buy you a billy goat.

And if that billy goat won't pull,
Mama's going to buy you a cart and bull.

And if that cart and bull turn over,
Mama's going to buy you a dog
named Rover.

And if that dog named
Rover won't bark,
Mama's going to buy you
a horse and cart.

And if that horse and cart fall down,
You'll still be the sweetest little baby
in town.

Girls and Boys Come Out to Play

Girls and boys come out to play,
The moon doth shine as bright as day,
Leave your supper and leave your sleep,
And join your playfellows in the street.
Come with a hoop, come with a call,
Come and be merry, or not at all,
Up the ladder and over the wall,
A penny loaf will serve us all.

Wee Willie Winkie

Wee Willie Winkie
Runs through the town,
Upstairs and downstairs
In his nightgown,
Rapping at the window,
Crying through the lock,
Are the children all in bed,
For it's past eight o'clock?

43

Hush-a-bye, Baby

Hush-a-bye, baby, on the tree top,
When the wind blows, the cradle will rock.
When the bough breaks, the cradle will fall,
Down will come baby, cradle and all.

Sleep, Baby, Sleep

Sleep, baby, sleep!
Thy father watches the sheep,
Thy mother shakes the dreamland tree,
And from it fall sweet dreams for thee.
Sleep, baby, sleep!

The Great Big Friend Hunt

Hannah Ray

Illustrated by Jacqueline East

Henry was a puppy.
A very small, very scruffy puppy.

He lived on a farm with Cleo the cat. Cleo was sleepy.
She never wanted to play with Henry.
Henry got very bored playing by himself.

When Henry was bored,
naughty things seemed
to happen.

And most of these
happened to poor Cleo.

"Oh, Henry," she sighed. "What you need is a friend. That would stop you from being bored."

Henry thought this sounded great. There was just one problem – what was a friend?

Henry headed into the yard where the other animals lived.
He stood up, straight and tall – as straight and as tall
as a small, scruffy dog can. In a loud voice he said,
 "I am going on a Friend Hunt.
A Great BIG Friend Hunt.
Will any of you help me?"

53

Douglas Donkey raised his head.
"Hee-haw! I'll help you, Henry,"
he said.

"Me, too," snorted Poppy the pig.

"And me!" mooed Clara the cow.

Henry was very happy with
all this help. But there was still one
problem – none of the other animals
knew what a friend was either!

Douglas Donkey decided to ask his daddy, who was very wise.

"A friend," said Douglas's daddy, "is someone to talk to."

Douglas Donkey trotted off
right away to tell Henry.

"Oh, thank you!" said Henry. "I'm so glad
you told me! Now we've found that out,
let's keep looking for a friend."

But they couldn't find one, and Henry
was starting to feel rather fed up.

Poppy asked her sister Petunia, who was very smart, if she knew what a friend was.

"Of course I do," replied Petunia.
"A friend cheers you up when you are sad."

"There you are!' exclaimed Poppy. "Now we know even more about friends. I'm sure we'll find one soon. Cheer up, Henry."

Henry felt much better.

But the animals still couldn't find a friend. Henry was beginning to worry that they were running out of time.

Clara's cousin, Camilla, had come to stay. She knew ever such a lot about ever so many things. When Clara asked her what a friend was she answered, "A friend is always happy to help."

With this in mind, the animals hunted
high and low – but it was no use.
They still couldn't find a friend...
and it was starting to get dark.

"Don't worry,
Henry," said
Clara. "We'll help
you look again
tomorrow. And the
day after that!"

"Oh, Cleo," sniffed Henry when they returned home. "We've hunted all day. We know a friend is someone to talk to. We know a friend cheers you up when you are sad. And we know a friend is always happy to help. But we just couldn't find one."

Cleo rolled her eyes, but she couldn't help smiling as she said, "A friend is someone to talk to? A friend cheers you up when you are sad? A friend is always happy to help?

You silly, small, scruffy dog!
You haven't just found one friend...

you've found lots!"

Said Mouse
to Mole

Clare Bevan

Illustrated by Sanja Rescek

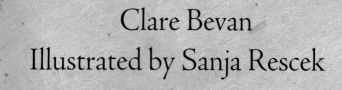

Said Mouse to Mole,
"How do you do?"

Said Mole to Mouse,
"And how are you?"

68

Said Mouse, "I'm feeling sad and blue."

Said Mole, "I'm feeling gloomy, too."

69

Said Mouse, "I wish that I could fly,
Like Bee and Bird across the sky."

Said Mole, "But if you fly around,
I'll miss you when I'm underground."

Said Mole, "I wish
that I could run,
Like Squirrel in the
summer sun."

72

Said Mouse, "But if
you play outside,
I'll miss you when I
have to hide."

Said Mouse, "I wish that I could float,
Like Beetle in his sailing boat."

74

Said Mole, "But if you sail away,
Who will talk to me all day?"

75

Said Mole, "I wish that I could sing,
Like Blackbird with his glossy wing."

76

Said Mouse, "But if you sing and shout,
The Big Bad Cat will prowl about!"

Said Mouse, "I wish that I could shine,
Like sunbeams in the summertime."

Said Mole, "But if
you're shiny bright,
The Big Bad Cat will
prowl all night."

Said Mole, "I wish that I could be
Taller than the tallest tree."

Said Mouse, "But if you grow so tall,
Your little house will be too small."

Said Mouse, "I wish that I could change
To something beautiful and strange."

Said Mole, "But if you're strange and new,
Will you like me? Will I like you?"

Said Mouse to Mole, said Mole to Mouse,
"Don't leave your home. Don't leave your house.
Don't be a snail. Don't be a star...

I LIKE YOU JUST THE WAY YOU ARE!"

Stroke the Cat

Stroke the cat,
stroke the cat
and lift it from the floor.

Stroke the cat,
stroke the cat
and shake hands with its paw.

Stroke the cat,
stroke the cat
and scratch its head once more.

Stroke the cat,
stroke the cat
– then **shoo** it through the door

In My Garden

There's a cat in my garden
with a wasp on her toes.
　　Shake it off,
　　shake it off.
Look,
　　there
　　　　it
　　　　　goes!   Wazzzzzzzzzzzzzzzzzzzzz

There's a dog in my garden
with a bee on his nose.
　　Shake it off,
　　shake it off.
Look,
　　there
　　　　it
　　　　　goes!   Buzzzzzzzzzzzzzzzzzzzzzzz

89

Playtime

Children creeping,
children peeping,
children leaping, leaping, leaping.

Children teasing,
children wheezing,
children sneezing, sneezing, sneezing.

Children calling,
children falling,
children bawling, bawling, bawling.

Children hopping,
Children flopping.

There goes the bell!

Children,
children,
children
stopping.

91

Climb the Mountain

Climb
the
mountain
high,
touch
the
clouds
and
see
the
sky.
Feel
the
wind
against
you
blow,
see

the
fields
far
far

below.

Animal Chat

Dogs growl,
Wolves howl.
Cows moo,
Doves coo.
Lions roar,
Crows caw.
Horses neigh,
Donkeys bray.
Monkeys shriek,
Mice squeak.
Parrots squawk
...and I talk.

93

My Dog's First Poem
(To be read in a dog's voice)

My barking drives them
   up the wall.
I chew the carpet
   in the hall.
I love to chase
   a bouncing...**banana**?

Everywhere I leave
   long hairs.
I fight the cushions
   on the chairs.
Just watch me race
   right up the...**shower**?

Once I chewed
a piece of chalk.
I get bored when
the family talk.
Then someone takes me
for a...**wheelbarrow**?

I'm a Rabbit

I'm a rabbit,
   rolled in a ball.

I'm a horse,
   jumping a wall.

I'm a mouse,
   nibbling at cheese.

I'm a dog,
   scratching its fleas.

I'm a hen,
   pecking at straw.

And I'm a cat,
   asleep on the floor.

The Autumn Leaves

In the autumn
the trees wave in the wind
and the leaves come
tumbling...

down,

down,

down,

down.

Here they come,
hundreds and thousands of leaves
in yellow, red,

hazel,

and

gold

chocolate brown.

A Week of Winter Weather

On Monday icy rain poured down
and flooded drains all over town.

Monday

Tuesday's gales bashed elm and ash,
dead branches came down with a crash.

Tuesday

On Wednesday bursts of hail and sleet.
No one walked along our street.

Wednesday

Thursday stood out clear and calm,
but the sun was paler than my arm.

Thursday

Friday's frost that bit your ears
was cold enough to freeze your tears.

102

Friday

Saturday's sky was ghostly grey.
We smashed ice on the lake today.

Saturday

Christmas Eve was Sunday... and
snow fell like foam across the land.

Sunday

Our Snowman

Wow, fatter and fatter and fatter he grows!
We give him button eyes and a red carrot nose.
He has a thick scarf for the North Wind that blows
and slippers to warm his cold toes,
      his cold toes,
        and slippers to warm
      his cold toes!

Up the Wooden Hill

Yawn!
to bed.
wooden hill
up the
going
sleepyhead,
dreamy
I'm a
Ted.
to one-armed
holding on
to bed,
wooden hill
Up the
Yawn!

104

Counting to Sleep

One. Two. Three. Four.
Five. Six. And Seven more.
Counting spiders,
counting flies,
counting rabbits,
   close
       your
           eyes...

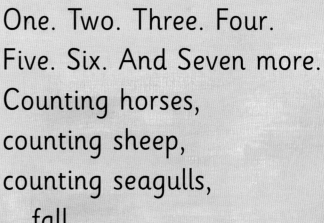

One. Two. Three. Four.
Five. Six. And Seven more.
Counting horses,
counting sheep,
counting seagulls,
   fall...
       asleep.

Wait for Me!

Written and Illustrated
by Eileen Browne

"I'm thirsty and hot,"
said Eddie the elephant.

"Me too," said Poppy
the parrot.

"So am I," said
Slippy the snake.

"I've got an idea!" said Molly the monkey.
"Let's go to the cool, sparkly river."

"Hooray!" said everybody.

"But how do we get to the cool, sparkly river?"
asked Eddie the elephant.

"It's easy!" said Poppy and Slippy and Molly.
"We cross the wide, sandy desert,
get past the huge pile of rocks,
push through the dark, tangly jungle,
and go over the green, slimy swamp.
That's how we get to the cool, sparkly river."

"Come on, follow us!"

They went to the wide, sandy desert.

"How can we cross it?"
asked Eddie the elephant.

"With a flap of my wings!" said Poppy.

"With a slither and a zigzag,"
said Slippy.

"With a hop and
a skip," said Molly.

"Let's go!"

Stomp, stomp, stompety-stomp, went Eddie the elephant.

"Wait for me!"

113

They reached the huge pile of rocks.

"How can we get past them?" asked Eddie.

"With a flap and a hop," said Poppy.

"With a wiggle and a squeeze,"
said Slippy.

"With a scramble and a climb," said Molly.

Puff-pant, puff-pant, went Eddie.

"Wait for me!"

They came to the dark, tangly jungle.

"How can we get through it?" asked Eddie.

"With a flutter and a flap," said Poppy.

"With a weave and a waggle," said Slippy.

116

"With a swing and a leap," said Molly.

Crash, smash, bumpity-bash, went Eddie.

"Wait for me!"

They got to the green, slimy swamp.

"How can we go over it?" asked Eddie.

"With a flap and a glide," said Poppy.

"With a slither and a wriggle," said Slippy.

"With a run and a slide," said Molly.

Squish, squelch, splatter and splodge,
went Eddie.

"Wait for me!"

At last, they arrived at the cool, sparkly river.

"Shall we fly in?" said Poppy the parrot.

"Shall we slip in?" said Slippy the snake.

"Shall we climb in?" said Molly the monkey.

"Go in how you like ... I'm JUMPING," said Eddie.

And Poppy and Slippy and Molly all shouted,

"Hey! Wait for me!"

Teddy's Birthday

Written by Anne Faundez
Illustrated by Karen Sapp

The toys are up early. What's happening today?
They bump and they bounce; they're ready to play.

Now they are gathered, it's time for some fun.
It's Teddy's birthday; today he is ONE!

"It's my BIRTHDAY!" cries Teddy,
"I hope everyone's ready!

It's party-time soon,
Let's decorate the room!"

Balloons all around, flowers everywhere,
A banner on the wall, streamers in the air.

"Oh, wow!" says Teddy.
"Party now! Are you ready?"

They clap to the music and make lots of noise,
Big Bear, Brown Bear — all of the toys.

Amanda the Panda and Jimmy Giraffe,
Together they dance and soon start to laugh.

Fluffy the Bunny has made lots of treats,
Biscuits and buns, ice cream and sweets.

Everyone's hungry. They each find a seat.
With tummies a-rumbling, they tuck in and eat.

Next, there's a cake on a big silver dish.
Teddy blows hard, and then makes a wish.

The toys clap their hands and together start singing.
Teddy is happy and cannot stop grinning.

"Happy Birthday to you,
Happy Birthday to you!
Happy Birthday, dear Teddy!
Happy Birthday to you!"

There's a gift for Teddy.
He's very excited.
A new bouncy ball!
He's truly delighted!

The toys are now yawning. Such sleepy heads!
They put on pyjamas and climb into bed.

After such an exciting and busy, busy day,
They close their eyes
And fall asleep...
straight away.

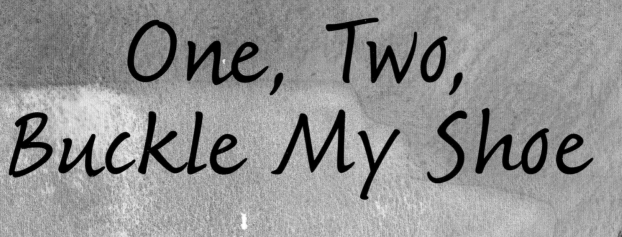

One, Two, Buckle My Shoe

Compiled by Anne Faundez
Illustrated by Brett Hudson

Hickory dickory dock,
The mouse ran up the clock.
The clock struck one,
The mouse ran down,
Hickory dickory dock.

Incy Wincy spider
Climbed up the water spout.
Down came the rain
And washed poor spider out.
Out came the sunshine
And dried up all the rain,
And Incy Wincy spider
Climbed up the spout again.

Higgledy, piggledy, pop!
The dog has eaten
   the mop;
The pig's in a hurry,
The cat's in a flurry,
Higgledy, piggledy, pop!

148

Oh, the grand old Duke of York,
He had ten thousand men,
He marched them up to the top of the hill,
And he marched them down again.

And when they were up,
  they were up,
And when they were down,
  they were down,
And when they were
  only halfway up,
They were neither up nor down.

I'm a little teapot, short and stout,
Here's my handle, here's my spout.
When I see the teacups, hear me shout,
Tip me up and pour me out!

Mary, Mary, quite contrary,
How does your garden grow?
With silver bells and cockleshells,
And pretty maids all in a row.

Hey, diddle, diddle,
The cat and the fiddle,
The cow jumped over
    the moon,
The little dog laughed
To see such sport,
And the dish ran away
    with the spoon.

154

Humpty Dumpty sat on a wall,
Humpty Dumpty had a great fall.
All the king's horses and all the king's men
Couldn't put Humpty together again.

Old MacDonald had a farm,
E-I-E-I-O!

And on that farm he had some pigs,
E-I-E-I-O!

With an oink oink here
and an oink oink there
here an oink
there an oink
everywhere an oink, oink!

Old MacDonald had a farm,
E-I-E-I-O!

And on that farm he had some ducks,
E-I-E-I-O!

With a quack quack here
and a quack quack there
here a quack
there a quack
everywhere a quack,
quack!

Old MacDonald had a farm,
E-I-E-I-O!

I had a little nut tree
And nothing would it bear
But a silver nutmeg and a golden pear.

The King of Spain's daughter came to visit me,
And all for the sake of my little nut tree.

I skipped over water, I danced over sea,
And all the birds in the air couldn't catch me.

The Queen of Hearts
She made some tarts,
All on a summer's day.
The Knave of Hearts
He stole those tarts,
And took them clean away.

One, two, buckle my shoe
Three, four, knock at the door
Five, six, pick up sticks
Seven, eight, lay them straight
Nine, ten,
A big fat hen!

Twinkle, twinkle little star,
How I wonder what you are.
Up above the world so high,
Like a diamond in the sky.
Twinkle, twinkle little star,
How I wonder what you are.

163

Lenny's
Lost Spots

Written by Celia Warren
Illustrated by Genny Haines

But in the afternoon, Lenny said,
"Where are my spots?
Where have they gone?
This morning I had six
but, now, I have none."

Lenny looked once.
Lenny looked twice.
He thought his spots
were on some dice.
But he was wrong.

Lenny looked down.
Lenny looked up.
He thought his spots
were on a pup.
But he was wrong.

172

Lenny looked high.
Lenny looked low.

174

He thought his spots were on a bow.
But he was wrong.

Lenny looked here.
Lenny looked there.
He thought his spots
were on a chair.
But he was wrong.

176

Lenny looked near.
Lenny looked far.
He thought his spots
were on a car.
But he was wrong.

178

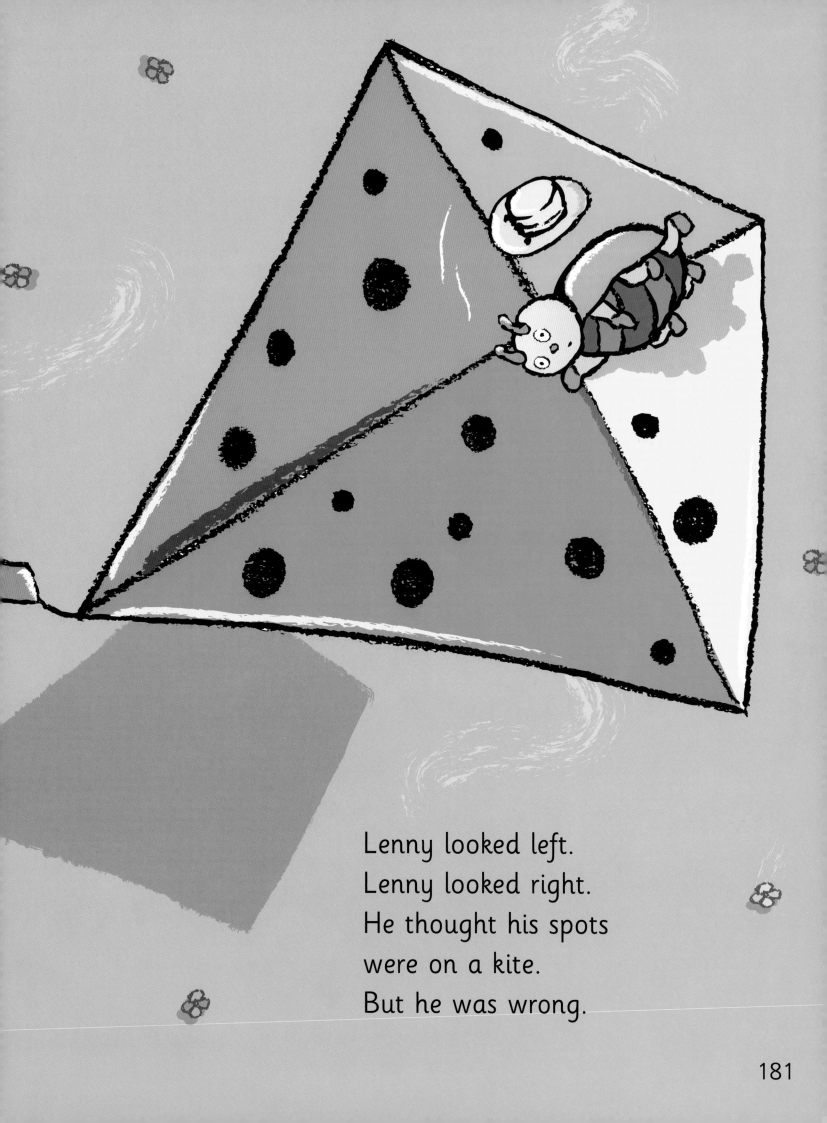

Lenny looked left.
Lenny looked right.
He thought his spots
were on a kite.
But he was wrong.

181

Lenny went out in the rain.
He said, "My spots are back again!"

And he was right.

183

Little Red Riding Hood

Written by Anne Faundez
Illustrated by Elisa Squillace

Once upon a time, there was a little girl who lived in a village near a forest. Her name was Little Red Riding Hood.

Do you know why she was called Little Red Riding Hood? It was because she had a beautiful red cloak with a hood, specially made by her granny.

The girl was very proud of her cloak
and she wore it all the time. So everyone
called her Little Red Riding Hood.

One day, Little Red Riding Hood's granny was ill in bed. Little Red Riding Hood helped her mother to bake some cakes for her granny.

"Little Red Riding Hood, take these cakes to your granny. Hurry along, now. Come home before the sun goes down, and don't talk to strangers," said Little Red Riding Hood's mother.

Little Red Riding Hood put the cakes in a basket and set off for her granny's cottage, on the other side of the forest.

Granny's House

The sun was high in
the sky, and sunlight
filled the forest.
Birds chattered in
the trees and little
creatures bustled
to and fro across
the path. Little
Red Riding
Hood was
very happy.

190

In the distance, Little Red Riding Hood saw a clearing full of bright blue and pink flowers. She wandered off the path towards them. Granny will love these flowers, she thought. She picked a large bunch and then continued on her way. By this time, the sun was low in the sky.

Suddenly, she heard a noise.
A scuffling, shuffling noise.
A big grey wolf stood in front of her.
 "Where are you going?" he asked.
 "I'm going to visit my granny.
She lives on the other
side of the forest and
she's not very well,"
replied Little Red
Riding Hood.

Little Red Riding Hood had forgotten that her mother had told her not to speak to strangers.

"I'd like to visit her, too," said the wolf. "You know what? You go your way and I'll take this path."
The wolf took a short cut.
Little Red Riding Hood continued on her way.

Now and then, Little Red
Riding Hood stopped
to pick more flowers.
By now, the sun had
set and the forest was
filled with shadows.

195

The wolf arrived at
Granny's house. He
knocked on the door.
Toc. Toc.

"Who's there?" asked
Granny.

"Little Red Riding Hood,"
replied the wolf, in a
squeaky voice.

"Lift the latch, my dear,
and come in," said Granny.

The wolf bounded into the room.
He pulled the old lady out
of bed and bundled her
into a wardrobe.

He jumped into her bed and tugged
the bedclothes up to his chin.

Little Red Riding Hood
arrived at her granny's
house. She knocked on
the door.
Toc. Toc.
  "Who's there?" said
a voice.
  "Little Red Riding
Hood," she answered.
  "Lift the latch, my
dear, and come in,"
called the voice.

Now, Little Red Riding Hood had never seen her granny ill in bed. She was astonished.

"Granny, what BIG arms you've got!" she said.

"All the better to hug you with, my dear," said the wolf.

"Granny, what BIG ears you've got!" she said.

"All the better to hear you with, my dear," said the wolf.

"Granny, what BIG eyes you've got!" she said. "All the better to see you with, my dear," said the wolf.

"Granny, what BIG teeth you've got!" she
said.
"All the better to **EAT** you with, my dear!"

And the wolf jumped out of bed and chased
Little Red Riding Hood around the room.

Just at that moment, by the light of the moon, a woodcutter was passing by. He heard a terrible banging and clanging coming from the cottage. He rushed inside and chased that wicked wolf right out of the forest and far away.

Little Red Riding Hood thanked the woodcutter. Then she unpacked her basket, and Granny, the woodcutter and Little Red Riding Hood sat down to a feast of cakes. And they all lived happily ever after.

The Jolly Rascal

Written by Clare Bevan

Illustrated by Angela Jolliffe

The Jolly Rascal sails away
Across the stormy sea,
With Captain Flo
And Big Bad Joe,
And pirates, one, two, three.

207

"Land ho! Land ho!"
 says Captain Flo.
"Let's look for gold," says Joe.
They flap, flap, flap
The treasure map,
The pirates say,
 "Let's go!"

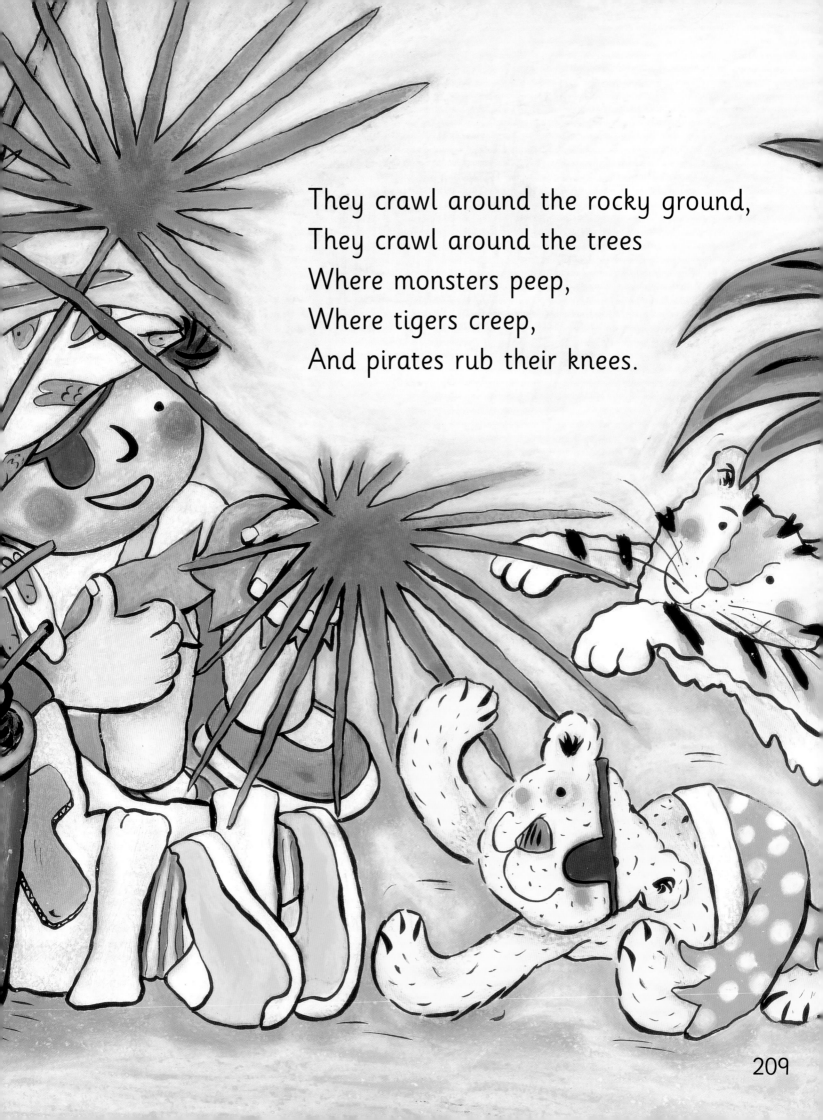

They crawl around the rocky ground,
They crawl around the trees
Where monsters peep,
Where tigers creep,
And pirates rub their knees.

"Away we go," says Captain Flo.
"Away we go," says Joe,
"With me and you,
With Tiger, too,
And pirates in a row."

They find a place where rivers race,
Where fishes swim about,
Where waters CRASH,
And ducks go SPLASH!
The pirates say, "Look out!"

They find a bay where people say,
"We're glad you came this way...
Here's food for you
And Tiger, too."
The pirates shout,
   "Hooray!"

213

"Follow me,"
   says Captain Flo.
"Follow me," says Joe,
"Past hut and hole
   and totem pole."
The pirates shout,
   "Bravo!"

They stamp their feet to a jungle beat,
They find a magic fountain.
Tiger passes
Stripy grasses
And pirates climb
 a mountain.

"Up we go!" says Captain Flo.
"Up we go!" says Joe,
"Climb so high
We touch the sky."
The pirates peer below.

216

They all look for
  a sandy shore,
They all look at the map...
Across the land
They spot the sand!
The pirates cheer and clap.

Says Flo to Joe,
"Sing yo, ho, ho!
The Jolly Rascal Song.
Dig far, dig low,
Dig fast, dig slow!"
The pirates sing along.

They dig the sand with spades
   and hands,
At last the treasure's here...
The golden rings,
The shiny things!
The pirates clap and cheer.

219

"Home we go,"
    says Captain Flo.
"Home we go," says Joe,
"With bags of gold
For us to hold."
The pirates sing,
    "Yo, ho!"

The Jolly Rascal sails away
From sand and land and tree,
With Captain Flo
And Big Bad Joe,
And pirates, one, two, three.

So Captain Flo
  and Big Bad Joe,
They cross the sea so deep.
In time for tea,
Then happily...
The pirates
  fall asleep.

Ready for a Picnic

Written by Celia Warren
Illustrated by Elke Zinsmeister

Grandma's Trip

Grandma packed her slippers,
her lipstick and her comb.
Grandma packed her
    toothbrush
and her bubble-bath foam.

Grandma packed her passport,
her bikini and some socks.
Grandma packed her camera
and her jewellery box.

Grandma packed her deckchair,
and a picnic hamper,
then, last of all, before she left,
Grandma packed...Grandpa!

I Like Eggs

Egg with sausage,
Egg with rice,
Egg with egg
If you like egg twice.

Egg with chips,
Egg on toast,
Egg on egg
If you like egg most.

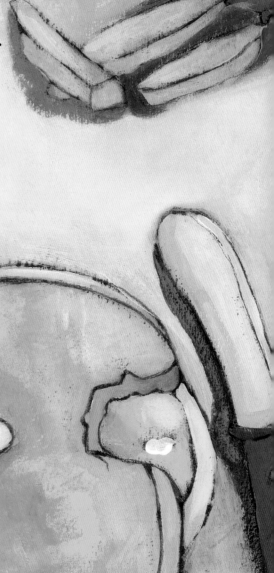

Ready for a Picnic

One for a sandwich,
Two for a cake,
Three for an ice cream by the lake.

Four for an apple,
Five for a pear,
Six for a picnic –
    see you there!

229

The Dizzy Hamster

"Tell me, little hamster, how does it feel
going round and round in your little wheel?"

"Well," said the hamster, "what I have found
is when the wheel stops, then the room goes round."

Giraffe

I'd like my head to be
   up in the blue,
Giraffe, giraffe, I'd like to be you.

I'd like to be as tall as a tree,
Giraffe, giraffe, would you
   like to be me?

I like the way you make
   funny faces,
Giraffe, giraffe, would you
   like to change places?

What Can I Be?

I can be a penguin and waddle as I walk,
I can be a parrot with a funny way to talk,
I can be a hamster and curl up small,
I can be a dog and bring you a ball,
I can be a monkey and swing from a tree
But, if you like, I can just be me.

Painting

I painted my daddy,
I painted my mummy,
But Mummy got cross
When I painted my tummy.

Off We Go

By the waterfall, then...

Up the hill

Roly-poly, roly-poly

Over the wall,

All

the

way

Along the road,

down.

Hats

Paper hats for parties,
Flowered hats for show,
Straw hats in summer,
Everywhere you go.

Hard hats for builders,
A white hat for a cook,
Wooly hats in winter,
Everywhere you look.

Riddles

The shape
of a plate or a
coin, the full moon
or a bowl of soup, the
shape of a button, the
sun or a wheel, what
shape is as round
as a hoop?

A
roof
or the shape
of the ear of a cat;
three sides and three
corners, what shape is that?

Landscape

My potato is an island.
The gravy is the sea.
The peas are people swimming.
The biggest one is me.

My carrots are whales
That make the sea wavy
But the big, brown blobs
Are LUMPS in the gravy!

Washing up

Knives and forks and spoons in a jumble,
Dishes clatter, splash and tumble,
Bubbles in the bowl where fingers fumble,
Doing the washing up.
SPLASH!

Ten Bold Pirates

Ten bold pirates,
    all ship-shape,
Two got sea-sick
    and that left eight.

Eight bold pirates
    up to their tricks,
Two met a shark
    and that left six.
Six bold pirates
    tired of being poor,
Two found treasure
    and that left four.

Four bold pirates
    feeling blue,
Two swam home again
    and that left two.

Two bold pirates
    drinking rum,
They fell asleep
    and that left none.

Garden Birds

Sparrow sings in the holly,
Starling sings in the oak.
Pigeon hops on the chimney pots,
Singing in the smoke.

Daffodil Dip

Dip, dip, daffodil,
Trumpet shout.
Dip, dip, daffodil,
You are OUT.

Dip, dip, daisy,
Petals all gone,
Dip, dip, daisy,
You are ON.

241

This Little Poem

This little poem,
You can keep in your hands.
Sometimes it wriggles,
And sometimes it stands.

It likes to wave,
It loves to clap,
Then it falls asleep,
face down in your lap.

The Wonderful Gift

Written by Clare Bevan
Illustrated by Kelly Waldek

When the little princess was born, the King and Queen were VERY excited.

"She will have EVERYTHING she wants," said the King.

"She will be the happiest princess in the whole world," said the Queen.

They gave her a golden rattle and a teddy bear with soft, silky fur. They rocked her in a silver cradle.

The little princess cried and cried and CRIED.

"Give the little princess a beautiful name," said the Wise Man. "Then she will be happy."
So the King and the Queen looked through a big book and chose the most beautiful name they could find.

"She will be called Princess Starlight," said the Queen. "Her room will be decorated with stars," said the King.

Princess Starlight cried and cried and CRIED.

One year later, Princess Starlight was STILL crying.
"Give her a birthday party," said the Wise Man.
"Everyone will bring her a present.
Then she will be happy."

So the King wrote letters on shiny paper to all the Fairy Godmothers. The Queen gave Princess Starlight a blue party dress, scattered with stars.

Princess Starlight cried and cried and CRIED.

It was a lovely party. There was a big
birthday cake with one candle and hundreds
of sugar stars. There were balloons shaped
like stars, and a mountain of presents
wrapped in starry paper.

"Now our little princess will be happy," said the King. "Now she will smile," said the Queen.

Princess Starlight looked at her cake and her balloons and her presents. She was quiet for a whole minute.

Then she started to CRY.

The Fairy Godmothers said, "We will give our presents to Princess Starlight. Then she will be happy."

They gave her a tiny flying horse, a talking mirror that could tell jokes, a crown made of moonbeams and a box of magic jewels.

Princess Starlight looked at
her presents for a long time.
Everyone held their breath.
Then she CRIED.

Many years went by.

Princess Starlight still wore beautiful dresses scattered with stars. Inside her starry room, she kept her magical presents.

Every day, jesters and jugglers tried to make her smile.

Every day, the King and Queen tried to make her happy.

But she STILL felt sad and wanted to cry.

One day, she heard
someone singing
outside her window.
"Who is THAT?"
she asked grumpily.

Princess Starlight stomped down the palace stairs to see the King and Queen. "Someone is making an AWFUL noise outside my window," she grumbled. "You must stop him at once."

"Of course," said the King and Queen. "If it will make you happy."

So the palace policeman found the singer and marched him indoors.

It was the gardener's son.
He looked very grubby,
but he had twinkly eyes.

259

"Why are you so happy?"
asked Princess Starlight crossly.

The gardener's son smiled. "Because the sun is shining and the flowers are growing," he answered.

"I don't understand," said Princess Starlight with a frown. "I have all my treasures, yet I feel sad."

"That is because you do not have the Wonderful Gift of Happiness," said the gardener's son.

"Where can we find this Wonderful Gift?" asked the King and Queen.

"Princess Starlight must find it for herself," said the gardener's son.

He led Princess Starlight outside and showed her how to dig in the earth. Together, they planted seeds and sang funny songs. They worked for many weeks.

One day, Princess Starlight ran indoors. She was grubby, but she was smiling and her arms were full of starry flowers.

"I still haven't found the Gift of Happiness," she laughed.

But, of course, she had. Hadn't she?

Katie's Mum is a Mermaid

Written by Hannah Ray
Illustrated by Dawn Vince

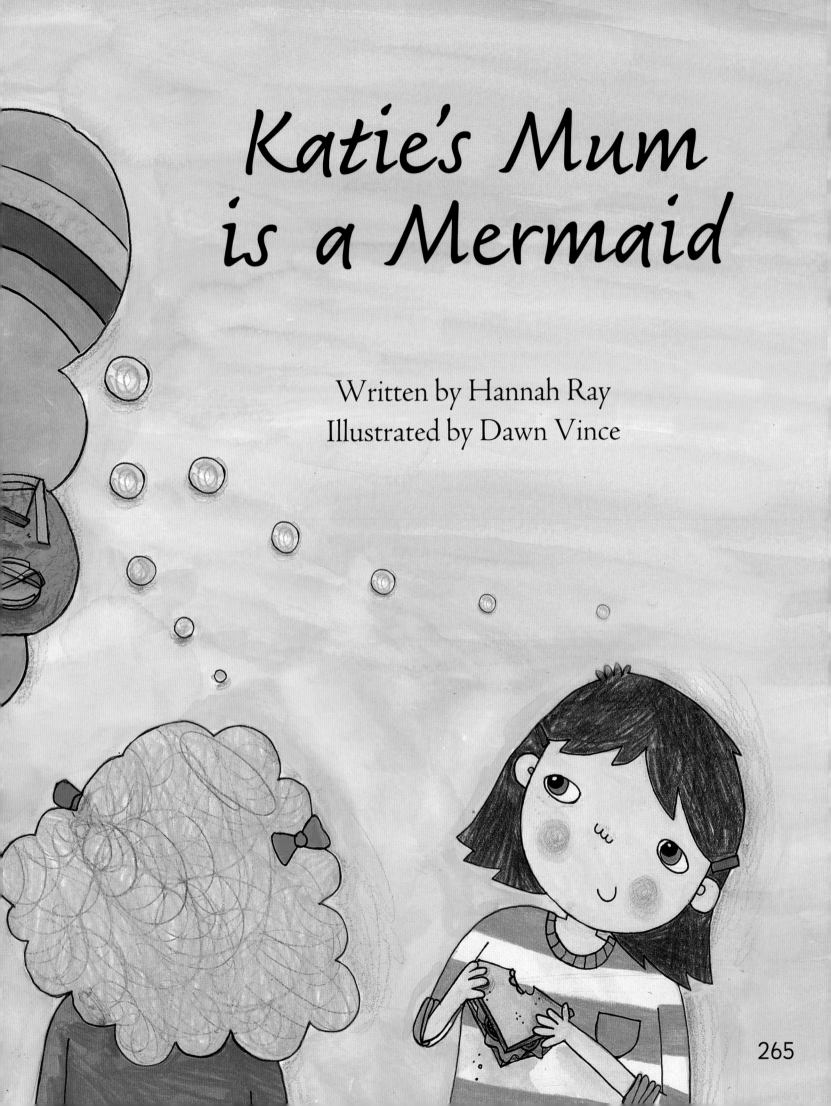

There's a new girl in my class,
Her name is Katie Pew,
Her hair is shiny, all golden curls,
Her eyes are sparkly blue.

Best friends with new girl Katie,
Is what I'd like to be,
But her life sounds so fantastic,
Would she be friends with me?

267

She says her mum's a mermaid,
Who sings in an ocean band.
An octopus plays the drum kit,
You can hear him on dry land.

Her dad's a famous cowboy,
Who rides a big white horse.
He gallops through the wild, wild west,
Catching outlaws, of course!

Katie's gran is a pilot,
Wearing goggles and a scarf.
She loops the loop and wiggles her wings,
To make the people laugh.

Her brother is a strongman,
Although he's only three,
Lifting elephants on one hand,
For all the world to see.

Katie's house is a castle,
With a drawbridge and a moat,
She says it gets quite chilly,
So she wears a giant coat.

There are butlers and a gardener,
A driver and a cook,
So grand it is, that Katie says,
The Queen came to take a look.

Last Friday Katie asked me,
To go around and play.
But after saying that I would,
She was quiet all day.

Katie led the way back home,
We wandered down the street.
I asked her where the castle was,
But she looked at her feet.

And when we got to Katie's house,
What a big shock I had!
A house like mine, with a bright red door,
Opened by Katie's dad.

A postman, not a cowboy,
Her dad delivers mail.
And Katie's mum, I soon found out,
Has legs and not a tail.

Katie's brother played with toys,
He showed me his best bear.
And her gran was just like my gran,
Though she did have bright pink hair!

But Katie still looked worried,
"I'm very sorry," she said.
She looked like she might start to cry,
Her face was very red.

Katie said, in a tiny voice,
"I told a fib or two,
But I wanted you to like me,
It's hard being brand new!"

But I am just like Katie,
I love to play pretend,
And now we are two princesses,
And are the best of friends!

Tiddalik the Frog

Written by Anne Faundez

Illustrated by Sanja Rescek

Long ago, in the Dreamtime, a huge red frog roamed the earth. His name was Tiddalik.

Tiddalik was so large that his back touched the sky. He was so wide that he filled the space between two mountain ranges. When he moved, the ground trembled and his feet made holes as big as valleys.

One day, he woke up from a very bad sleep.
He was VERY, VERY grumpy!
He was also VERY, VERY thirsty!

"Water! Water!" he bellowed.
His words made the clouds crackle with thunder

He found a river and drank up all the water.
He found a lake and emptied that, too.
He kept on drinking until every waterhole was dry.

Tiddalik was now bulging with
water and ready to burst.

He was too uncomfortable
to move. He shut his
eyes and fell into a
long, deep sleep.

The days went by.

Tiddalik slept.

There was no sign of rain in the skies.

The sun scorched the earth. The grasses withered and the trees lost their leaves.

The beautiful green earth became hard and cracked.

Kangaroo, Kookaburra and Platypus
were anxious. They had watched
Tiddalik drinking up all the water.
Now their land was turning to dust.

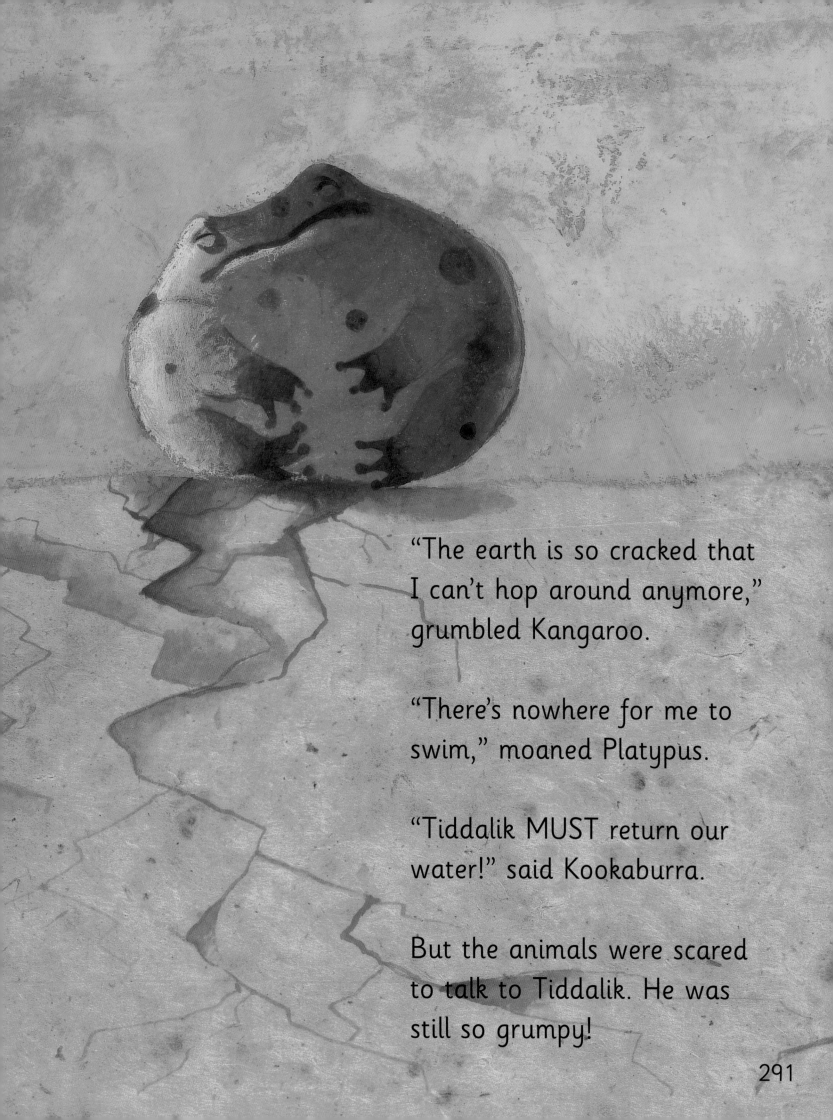

"The earth is so cracked that I can't hop around anymore," grumbled Kangaroo.

"There's nowhere for me to swim," moaned Platypus.

"Tiddalik MUST return our water!" said Kookaburra.

But the animals were scared to talk to Tiddalik. He was still so grumpy!

"I know," said Kookaburra.
"Let's make him laugh. Then
he'll spill out the water."

So Kookaburra flew right up to
Tiddalik. She sang some funny
songs. She wiggled and jiggled
and danced around.

Tiddalik opened one eye.
He shut it again.

Platypus went up to Tiddalik. She told a few jokes and then she flipped and flopped and shuffled around.

Tiddalik opened the other eye.
He shut it again.

Next, it was Kangaroo's turn.
He loved to show off.
He twirled and whirled,
and thumped and
bumped his tail around.

Tiddalik opened both eyes.
He shut them again.
He was still bored.

Just then, Little Eel came rushing towards the animals.

"Let me make Tiddalik laugh!"
he cried.

He raced towards
Tiddalik, turning
somersaults all
the way.

Little Eel landed on Tiddalik's bulging stomach.
He scrambled to get himself upright.
He teetered and tottered and then stood,
looking up at the gigantic frog.

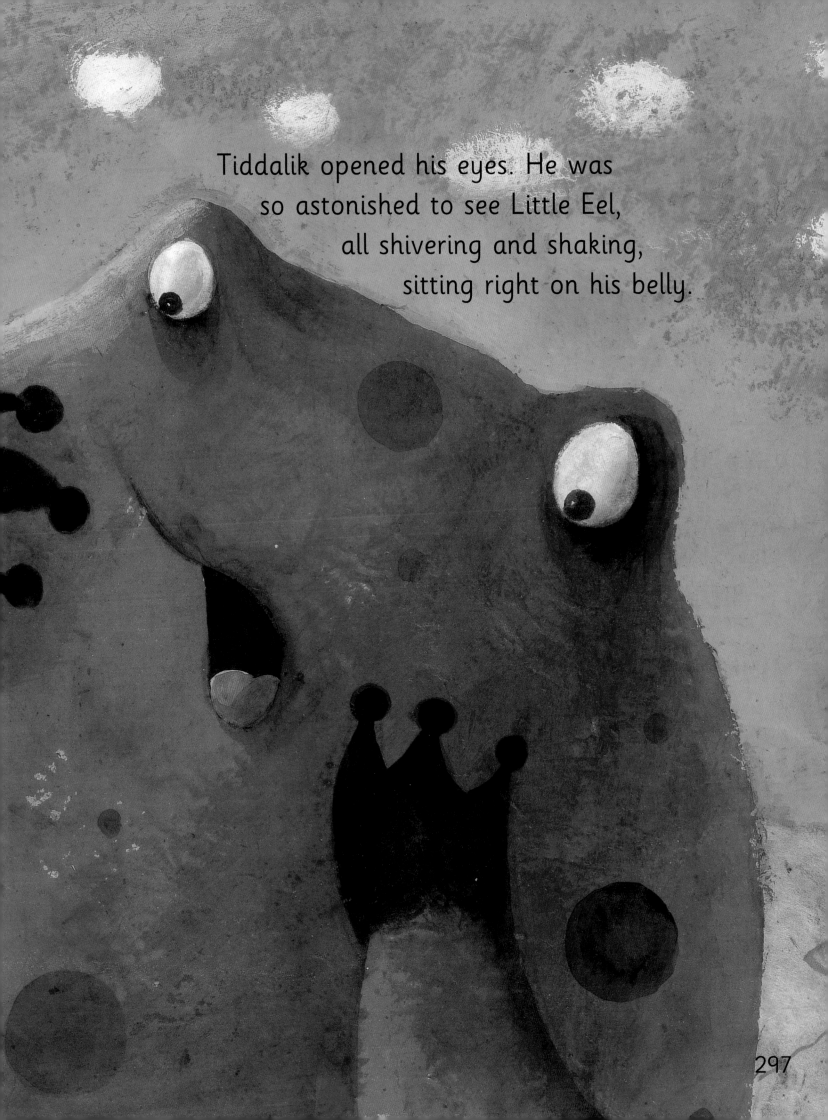

Tiddalik opened his eyes. He was
so astonished to see Little Eel,
all shivering and shaking,
sitting right on his belly.

Tiddalik made a rumbling noise.
He chuckled – and a trickle of water
dribbled from his mouth.

He chuckled some more.

Soon, he was rumbling with laughter.
Water spilled from his mouth and ran down his sides.
Tiddalik couldn't stop laughing at the sight of
Little Eel sitting on his belly.
As he laughed, he felt less grumpy.

Soon, the land was awash with water.
The grasses began to grow again, and tiny leaves
began to cover the bare branches of the trees.

And do you know what? To this day, Tiddalik
has never again emptied the land of water.

Why?

CONTENTS

~

KU-613-220

INTRODUCTION

When I first saw a piece of dough modelling I could not believe that something so appealing and apparently so enduring could be made from what was, basically, food. I was captivated by a gorgeous little rustic doll that a friend had hanging in her kitchen – it had been left mainly dough coloured, with just its rosy cheeks and some parts of the clothing painted. It was charming.

The doll was a gift brought from some remote part of the country and, needless to say, no-one knew how it was made. As an artist, nothing gets my creative juices flowing more quickly than the prospect of working with new materials, so, totally inspired, I called into the library on my way home confident of finding a book that would reveal the secret of the dough. There was no such book – not in the library, the book shop nor the craft shop; not under the counter nor on the black market; not on friends' bookshelves;

not even to be purchased by post! I am known for my tenacity and I wanted to know how to model dough. I wanted to know exactly what was in the recipe, whether it was cooked and, if so, for how long and at what temperature. What type of paint was on it? Did it need varnishing?

I began a quest for information and no-one was spared from interrogation. Casual conversations started at parties, on trains or in bus queues were gradually worked around to the subject of dough modelling and its complexities but all to no avail. If anyone knew anything, they were keeping very quiet about it. At the end of two years of dedicated questioning, I was none the wiser about the secret practices of dough modellers except for one slender clue: there had been several references to pieces seen abroad, with particular mention of pieces from America, Germany and various Scandinavian countries. I

Decorative DOUGH

~

Joanna Jones

Dealerfield

To my family and friends,
especially the Governor

Published in 1993 by Merehurst Limited, Ferry House,
51–57 Lacy Road, Putney, London SW15 1PR

This edition specially printed for Dealerfield Ltd 1995

ISBN 1 85927 065 4

A catalogue record of this book is available from the British Library.

Edited by Bridget Jones
Designed by Maggie Aldred
Photography by James Duncan
Styling by Madeleine Brehaut

Typeset by Rowland Phototypesetting Limited,
Bury St Edmunds, Suffolk

Colour Separation by Fotographics, UK – Hong Kong
Printed and Bound in China by Leefung-Asco Printers Limited.

therefore decided to target people with foreign accents and – although it slowed down my investigations considerably and, as you might imagine, led to some bizarre misunderstandings – this eventually paid off.

My family had long since closed ranks against my obsession and banned any public manifestations of it in their presence. Despite this, I had arranged our Christmas shopping so that a bit of dough research in Harrods' book department went almost unnoticed. As I managed to conduct what was surely a fruitless search among the craft books, I overhead the remnants of a conversation and picked up an unmistakeable American accent. I turned to see an exasperated American man darting between the bookshelves and a large lady in a wheelchair. He was on the point of exploding as his latest offering, a weighty craft book, was again rejected. 'The fact of the matter is,' he hissed, 'you've done every craft known to man.'

This lady had all the attributes of a perfect interviewee – she was American, she had 'done every craft known to man' and she was unable to escape. I seized my chance and made general conversation on a diversity of crafts, such as American quilting and British barge painting, before asking her The Question. 'Have you ever done any dough modelling?' I tried to make it sound as casual as the rest of the conversation but I could hardly contain my excitement and the words seemed to hang in the air for hours before she answered: 'Heck, yes, masses of it'.

I scrabbled in my bag for an old envelope and a pencil as my new-found friend looked across to her husband, who had defected to the section on sports books, settled herself back in her chair, then proceeded to enlighten me on the alchemy that transformed mere dough into an art.

egg glaze in this section. This gives any dough which is to be left unpainted a marvellous, rich colour and sheen when baked.

NOTE

● You will see that the recipe quantities are expressed as follows for each project:
8 flour × 4 salt × 2 paste.
The figures indicate the number of tablespoons required.

12 tablespoons plain (all-purpose) white
    flour = 175g (6oz/1½ cups)

16 tablespoons plain (all-purpose) white
    flour = 250g (8oz/2 cups)

8 tablespoons salt = 175g (6oz/1 cup)

12 tablespoons salt = 280 g (9oz/1½ cups)

● Where wallpaper paste is used it should be measured when mixed with water according to the manufacturer's instructions. The quantities used in the basic recipes give an average amount of dough suitable for most projects.

· ORIGINAL DOUGH ·

This is the recipe which the American woman gave me.

500g (1lb) plain (all-purpose) white flour
250g (8oz) 8 tablespoons salt
25g (8 fl oz) cold water

1 Thoroughly mix the flour and salt in a bowl.

2 Stir half the water into the flour mixture, then draw the dough together and continue to add water gradually until the dough is pliable enough to knead. If the mixture is too crumbly,

continue adding the water drop by drop. You will know the dough is ready when it is firm enough not to stick your hands but not so dry that it is crumbly.

3 Turn the dough out on a smooth surface and continue to knead it for at least 10 minutes. The dough has been kneaded sufficiently when it is smooth, pliable and very slightly warm.

· PASTE DOUGH ·

This mixture will seem slightly sticky while you are making it but it should become smooth and warm when kneaded. It has a texture which is a little more elastic than the Original Dough.

45g (1½oz) wallpaper paste
375g (12oz) plain (all-purpose)
white flour
375g (12oz) salt
185ml (6 fl oz) cold water

1 Mix the wallpaper paste with water, if necessary, following the manufacturer's instructions and observe any suggested standing time.

2 Mix the flour and salt in a bowl, then add the wallpaper paste. Proceed as for the Original Dough, step 2.

GOLDEN EGG · GLAZE ·

Simply beat an egg with 1 tablespoon water and paint it on the dough before baking. Be sure not to glaze anything

which you intend to paint later, as paint will not take smoothly over glazed dough.

One application of glaze will give a beautifully golden dough but you may repeat the process every 20 minutes or so during baking for a darker colour.

Before You Start

Here are some very basic helpful – or rather essential – hints to read before you begin working with dough.

● As dough does not keep successfully in the refrigerator, becoming stretchy and unmanageable, make only as much as you need for the project in hand.

● Do not grease or flour the baking sheet.

● While you are working, keep any spare dough under a damp tea towel to prevent it from drying out. Do not wrap it in plastic wrap or foil as this will make it sticky and unworkable.

● Shape the dough directly on the baking sheet as you will ruin your model if you try to move it when it is complete.

● Always roll out dough on a lightly floured board. It can be difficult to explain how thick the dough should be and to measure it exactly for every project, so, unless I have specified otherwise, 'thin dough' means about the same thickness as you would use for pie crust and 'very thin' means about half that thickness. With practice you will soon be able to gauge the depth by eye.

● Make sure that the knife is sharp when cutting dough and use a well-floured plastic ruler to cut straight edges.

- Always dampen the dough before joining two pieces. Use an artist's paint brush rather than a pastry brush which is too big.
- Use only cotton stamens as some of the other types do not fare well in the oven. They can be painted easily and varnished after the dough has been baked.
- The dough must be thoroughly dried out at the end of baking and it should feel dry and hard. Although times are given at the end of every project these can only be approximate as there are so many variables to dough modelling, such as the thickness of your model or the moistness of your dough.

Different ovens cook at different speeds and you may find that using a fan oven will also effect the time your model takes to cook. If the top of your model appears to be cooked but the back remains stubbornly damp or even stuck, remove it carefully from the sheet with a long bladed knife and then retun it to the oven upside down on a bed of crumpled foil.

- To test if a thick model is baked sufficiently, insert a fine needle in through the back of the dough: if this goes in very easily and comes out looking smeared, then the piece should be returned to the oven, placed upside down as above.
- Leave the cooked dough to cool completely on a wire rack before completing the decoration.

Basic Techniques

KNEADING

As soon as all the ingredients are well bound together, tip the ball of dough out on a lightly floured smooth surface. Take hold of the dough in both hands, then press down and push it away from you with the base of your palms. Alternate this action with a sideways folding movement to keep the ball of dough to roughly the same size and shape as it is kneaded. Continue kneading for at least 10 minutes, by which time the dough should be smooth and very slightly warm. It is essential to knead dough firmly and for the recommended time to avoid problems when modelling.

ROLLING ROPES

Roll a piece of well-kneaded dough into a rough sausage shape on a lightly floured board. Place the fingers of both hands together in the middle of the sausage and work them out towards the ends rolling the dough backwards and forwards. Repeat until the rope is the required length and thickness. By using your fingers rather than the palms of your hands, you exert less pressure and have more control, and your rope is more likely to be of even thickness when finished.

MAKING A TWIST

Lay two ropes of the same length side by side. Starting in the centre, twist them around each other, then work outwards, first to one end, then to the other. Fix

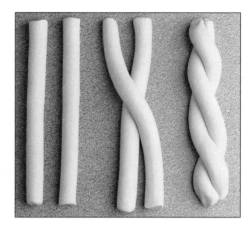

Making a twist.

the ropes together at both ends. By working from the middle, you are less likely to make a twist with one thick end and one thin end.

WEAVING DOUGH

Roll out a large piece of dough to the required thickness. Using a well-floured plastic ruler and a sharp knife, cut the dough into as many strips as you need. Most bowls and baskets take about ten strips.

Place two strips of dough one over the other in the form of a cross. Lay a third strip parallel to the bottom strip and over the second one. Weave a fourth strip over the last strip and under the bottom first strip. Continue weaving alternate vertical and horizontal strips, until you have a section large enough for your project. It is easier to weave strips under if you fold the top strips back, then replace them afterwards.

There is not usually any need to fix the strips with water but it is sometimes necessary as you complete a section when working on a particularly steep-sided dish or bowl.

Weaving dough: it is easier to weave strips under if you fold top strips back.

MAKING HAIR

Dough is extruded through a garlic press, clay gun or fine sieve, such as a nylon tea strainer, to make hair. Whichever method you use, try to give your figure a recognizable style rather than leaving the dough in a tangled mess. However, avoid wispy fly-away arrangements as they tend to break off – giving 'split ends' a whole new meaning.

Garlic Press Fill the press with a ball of dough, then push it through the holes. If the resultant strands are long enough, cut them off using a sharp knife. For longer strands, recharge the press with dough, before cutting the first batch off and push it through. Wet the head, then, if possible, use plastic tweezers to transfer the hair in single strands.

Clay Gun Fit one of the sieve-like discs into the end of the gun and load with a roll of dough which has been slightly softened with a little water. Push a length of dough through the gun on to a very lightly floured board. Using floured plastic tweezers, pick up little clumps of hair and arrange them on the dampened head.

Clay-gun hair is very fine. With care it can be extruded in small waves directly on the head; alternatively, arrange it with the tweezers, then push it up into curls and waves using a cocktail stick (toothpick) or modelling tool.

Fine Sieve I use this method for very fine hair for a doll, a short curly boy's style or for a permed effect. Soften the dough slightly and use the back of a wooden spoon to push it through a sieve. The longer you work with the spoon, the

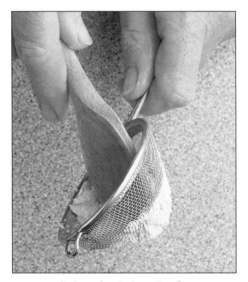

Pushing dough through a fine sieve to make hair.

longer the hair will grow on the other side of the sieve; however, generally speaking, this is a method for making short hair. Remove the hair from the sieve with a sharp knife and transfer it directly to the head.

MODELLING HANDS

Lay two suitable ropes of dough side by side on a floured board. Flatten the ends closest to you with a finger, then use a sharp knife to cut a small triangle of dough from the inside edge of each of the flattened pieces to represent the space between the thumb and the first finger.

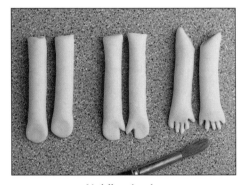

Modelling hands.

Make three small cuts along the bottom edge of each piece to represent the fingers and trim these to the appropriate lengths. Using the sharp knife or a damp paint brush, carefully round the ends of the fingers and thumbs.

MAKING A BOW

Cut two long, narrow strips of dough. Cut a quarter of the length from one and cut the other in half diagonally. Take the diagonally cut pieces and notch both the straight ends before fixing the diagonal ends together, on the piece to be decorated.

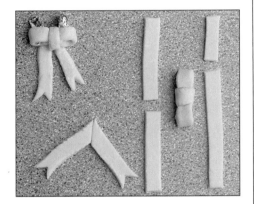

Making a bow.

Loop both ends of the longest remaining piece towards the middle and fix together in the centre. Wrap the last short piece around the middle to represent the knot and fix together at the back. Arrange the bow in the centre of the ribbon tails. Fill the loops with some crushed silver foil, if necessary, to support their shape during baking.

MAKING A FRILL
Use a 7.5cm (3in) round fluted cutter to cut out a circle of thinly rolled dough. Use the medium ring from the rose cutter set to remove the centre of the circle.

Use a cocktail stick (toothpick) like a very small rolling pin to roll out each of the flutes around the edge of the circle. Flour the cocktail stick repeatedly while you work, gently using a slightly rocking

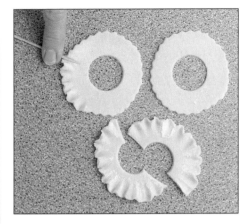

Making a frill.

movement. When you have frilled all around the circle, cut it into the required lengths.

A SITTING CAT
Make two slim ropes of dough for the front legs and place them side by side on a floured board. Make three small cuts along the front edge of both to represent the toes. Round each of these individually with a damp paint brush. Trim the other end of each leg diagonally and fix together with a little water.

Place a small pear-shaped piece of dough on top of the legs, tapered end to the front, so that about half the legs are still protruding. Make a small ball of dough for the head and add a very small triangular wedge of dough for a nose. Add two very small, flattened balls of dough close to the nose, to represent whisker pads. Fix the head in place. Make two pointed ears by cutting a small circle with a rose cutter and quartering it. Flatten two of these quarters a little and

fit them to the top of the cat's head.

Fix a thin, tapering rope of dough on the rear of the cat, then curl it around the body. Cut a very narrow strip from some rolled-out dough and arrange this around the cat's neck. Add a bow.

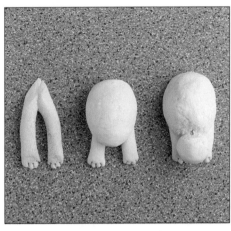

Making a sitting cat.

NOTE
● If you want to attach the cat's head at a particularly awkward angle, water alone is not enough to keep it in place. Take a short length of wire and push half into the body and the other half into the head.

MAKING A BUTTERFLY
Using the butterfly cutter, stamp the shape out of thinly rolled dough and fix it on the project with a little water. Roll a very small cigar-shaped body and fix this between the two wings. Wet the sides of the body a little and push the wings up so that they adhere to it enough to hold them up. If the wings droop, then support them during baking with two small rolls of foil. Trim two black stamens to the right length and push

these into the front of the body to represent antennae.

If you want to make a really fancy butterfly you can make small cuts into the edges of the wings and roll them with a floured wooden skewer, as for the Carnation petals, see page 13.

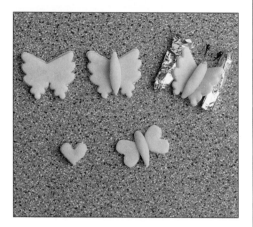

Making a butterfly.

To make a small butterfly, cut out two small hearts. Trim off the pointed ends of the hearts and stick them on either side of a small cigar-shaped body. Paint antennae on small butterflies at a later stage.

MODELLING A BIRD

Take a small ball of well-kneaded dough and pull out one side slightly. Model this into a rounded head with a pinched-in neck and a small beak. Flatten the opposite end of the dough into a fan-shaped tail and pinch this in at the base. Tip the tail up slightly and make three or four small cuts along the edge to represent tail feathers. Use a small leaf cutter to make two wings and feather these with the back of your knife. Finish by indenting two eyes using a cocktail stick (toothpick).

MAKING A TEDDY

Model two short, thin ropes of dough with feet as for the Victorian Girl, see page 34. Trim the other ends of the legs diagonally.

For the body, mould a small ball of dough into an egg shape and flatten it slightly where the arms and legs are going to be attached. Sit the body up on a baking sheet or in position on a model and attach the legs to the appropriate flattened areas. Make two more thin, short ropes of dough for arms and cut a little notch in one end of each to represent thumbs. Trim the other ends diagonally and fit these in place on the body. Arrange the paws against the body.

For the head, mould a small ball of dough into a rounded pyramid shape. Take the more pointed end for a snout and fix a small triangular piece of dough on the end for a nose. Flatten two very

Making a teddy.

small balls of dough and fix these close to the nose to represent whisker pads. Make two more small balls of dough into small saucer-shaped ears by pressing with the rounded end of a modelling tool. Fix these in position and add a bow on the neck.

MAKING LEAVES WITHOUT CUTTERS

Press a small fresh leaf into the rolled-out dough, then use nail scissors to cut around the impression which it leaves. This will give realistic veining and works wonderfully with short and odd-shaped leaves, such as those from primroses.

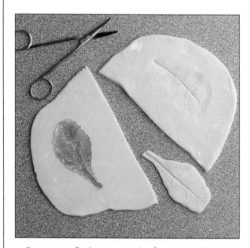

Pressing a fresh primrose leaf into dough to leave an impression which may be cut out.

Long tapering leaves, like those on daffodils are best made by cutting them out freehand with a sharp knife, then adding a long central vein afterwards. If they do go a bit crooked, it doesn't matter as this only adds to the sense of realism.

Veining Leaves Use the back of a knife to mark the veins in leaves which are stamped out using cutters. Mark a central vein and four or five pairs of small veins coming from it.

MAKING ROSES

I generally use the two smallest cutters in the rose set. Cut out two small circles and two larger ones from thinly rolled dough. Cut all the circles in half and flatten them slightly to make the edges as thin as possible. Take one of the smaller halves and, starting at one corner, roll the semi-circle of dough into a coil so that it resembles the centre of a rose. Fix the end with a little water. You may leave some pieces at this stage to represent rosebuds.

Dampen the longest edges of the remaining three small semi-circles before

Making roses: one rolled semi-circle makes a bud, four semi-circles make a small rose and eight semi-circles make the full bloom.

wrapping them evenly around the bud, overlapping them to make them fit. At this stage, the roses may be used as small, or half-opened, flowers. Add the final four large semi-circles in the same way.

Making a Rose Without Cutters Flatten two small and two larger balls into circles, then use as above.

MAKING CARNATIONS

Using a carnation cutter set, cut one of each size of circles from thinly rolled dough and lay them on a well-floured board. Use a sharp knife to make three short cuts in each of the flutes on every circle. Use a well-floured wooden skewer to roll out each flute with a short rocking movement to make them slightly ragged and frilled like the edges of fresh carnation petals.

Dampen the middle of each circle, then stack them with the largest at the bottom and the smallest on top. Pick up all the petals together and pinch them together from underneath so that they make a flower shape before you fix them in position.

Making a Carnation Without Cutters Cut out a circle of dough with a small round fluted cutter, then snip the flutes and roll them using a well-floured skewer in the same way as above.

Fold the circle in half, then in half again to make a triangle or wedge shape with all the frills at the top. Trim off the pointed end of the triangle and fix the flower in position before carefully opening out and arranging the petals to look more realistic.

Making carnations: the cut-out shapes are frilled and stacked, the skewer may be pushed through the centre before pinching the petals together at the back.

MOULDING VIOLETS

Fit a small ball of dough over the pointed end of a wooden skewer to cover the top 6mm (¼in) without breaking through the dough.

Make four or five cuts in the bottom edge of the dough to make three or four

Making violets.

13

strips and one wider one. With the dough still on the end of the skewer, carefully lift each of the strips and press them between your finger and thumb, bending them outwards like petals at the same time.

Remove the violet from the skewer and shape the petals a little more with your fingers before arranging it on your model.

MAKING DAFFODILS
Work directly on the model as a daffodil is impossible to pick up once made. Using a daffodil cutter set, take the smaller of the two petal cutters and cut five petals from thinly rolled dough. Arrange these in a circle with their ends touching in the middle.

Cut out the trumpet. Working on a floured board, make several small cuts along the longest edge with a knife, then use a well-floured wooden skewer to roll the edge gently so that the dough

Making daffodils.

becomes more splayed and ragged. Carefully roll the trumpet around the skewer so that the short edges meet and fix them together with a little water. Pinch the unfrilled end of the tube together and fix the trumpet into the middle of the petal circle.

Making Daffodils Without Cutters
Daffodils can be made without cutters, simply by making a card template for the petals and cutting the rectangular piece straight instead of curved. Use nail scissors to cut the dough.

MAKING HANGING HOOKS
The most successful hanging hooks are made from traditional hairpins. Trim them to length, as necessary for your project, using wire cutters. The trimmings from the straight-sided pins may be bent into hooks as well.

Painting and Varnishing

Painting dough models is every bit as exciting as making them. It is amazing how you can transform even the most primitive piece of modelling into something approaching a work of art with a little painterly care and attention.

To get the best results you have to be prepared to use the right materials, so forget any ideas you might have about raiding the children's paint boxes or using that small dogs-body of a paint brush lurking in the kitchen drawer. You will need some good-quality, water-

based paints, two or three decent paint brushes, a palette and some varnish, all of which you will find in your local art shop in such bewildering variety that it might be helpful if I tell you which is which and why I use the ones that I do.

You will definitely need a palette of some kind and the best ones are made of china, with several mixing sections around a central well to resemble a flower. Plastic palettes tend to discolour with use. If all else fails, saucers and plates make good substitutes but as you quite often need to mix up large quantities of runny paint, a proper palette keeps the colours separated more effectively.

Absorbent kitchen paper is very handy, both for laying your model on while you are working and for wiping your brushes. I also keep a sharp craft knife and some cotton buds by me in case I make a mistake and get some paint on a part that I have decided to leave dough coloured, then I can either wipe it off or scrape it away.

WATER COLOURS
These come in small cakes or in little tubes. This type of paint is intended to be used transparently and you will have to use a great deal of it, and many layers, to achieve the opaque finish usually associated with dough modelling. However, I do use it sometimes if I want to preserve the look of the natural dough with just an occasional, gentle wash of colour. It gives the piece a slightly

antique look and is especially nice on small Victorian-type items.

ACRYLIC PAINTS

In my opinion, acrylic paints are not suitable for dough modelling because their natural tendency to dry quickly is accentuated by the porous quality of the dough. This prevents any possibility of blending the paint as well as causing patchiness on plain colours. This can be alleviated, to some extent, by first sealing the dough with some form of undercoat but the results do not justify the effort.

CRAFT PAINTS

These are little pots of ready-mixed paints for craft workers. They are fine for dough and are especially good if you do not have confidence in your own ability to mix colours. They can be used in opaque form or it is possible to water them down to a transparent consistency, although this will not have the delicacy of water colours. Craft paints can be mixed together but care must be taken to avoid a 'muddy' result.

POSTER PAINTS

Your children probably use poster paints and, although it is quite possible to use them on dough, usually the results tend to be rather garish and powdery.

GOUACHE PAINTS
OR DESIGNERS' COLOURS

These are the paints that I use because they really are the most perfect, and versatile, paints for dough modellers. I usually use Winsor and Newton paints and most of the names on the colour chart relate to this make. Gouache is available in all the earth colours and pure hues, making mixing and blending relatively easy. It dries at a reasonable rate and can be watered down to a transparent wash which is nearly as good as water colour.

BRUSHES

As a painter I would always advise you to buy the best brushes that you can afford; in the case of dough modelling, a very good, round, sable brush with a decent point. However, the rough surface of baked dough is very hard on brushes so it wears out sable quickly. Unfortunately, synthetic brushes lose their points speedily. The solution is to invest in one small, size 1, sable brush for all your fine work and two larger synthetic brushes, sizes 2 and 3, which you will probably use more often and where having a good point for fine work is not essential. To preserve the all-important points on all your brushes, do not leave them in your water jar while you are working.

VARNISH

Because dough contains so much salt it is very susceptible to damp, which softens and, eventually, ruins it. Therefore it has to be varnished with quite strong varnish to seal it. Unfortunately, the stronger the varnish, the more likely it is to tint the work yellow which does not matter very much on natural dough or dark colours but it does dull the clarity of the colour a little on light and pastel shades.

A good-quality clear gloss, oil based, polyurethane varnish is best and you will find that the sparkle varnishing gives your work usually compensates for any slight yellowing. Although one coat of varnish will do if you want to preserve a pale colour it is best to apply several coats, both back and front. It is also advisable to use a stronger sealant, such as yacht varnish, on bowls or other pieces that are going to be used and handled a lot. Since this type of varnish gives a more yellow finish, it is sensible to use darker colours when painting such pieces.

Keep a small soft brush solely for applying varnish and always clean it in turpentine or white spirits (mineral spirits), then rinse it in warm soapy water before you put it away.

Being very porous, dough will take a generous coat of varnish so check for drips and runs before you leave it to dry. Varnish usually takes 24 hours to dry completely and it is advisable to leave it this long between coats.

PAINTS USED FOR PROJECTS

	Fruit Bowl	Daffodil Bowl	Primrose Basket	Strawberry Basket	Victorian Wreath	Fruit Garland	Flower Garland	Fruit Wreath	Victorian Girl	George	Catherine Sheep	Heathcliff Pig	Finley Fish	Claude	Nursery Window	Cat Napping	Twisted Floral Initial	Clown Initial	Initial with Figure	Love Birds Heart	Entwined Hearts	Mother's Day Dish
Yellow Ochre															●							
Cadmium Yellow									●	●								●	●			
Lemon Yellow		●	●				●										●					
Golden Yellow	●	●		●	●	●	●	●												●		
Linden Green	●					●		●														
Sap Green		●												●		●						
Viridian													●									
Permanent Green Middle																						
Olive Green	●		●	●	●	●	●	●							●		●			●	●	●
Ultramarine					●		●		●	●	●		●	●	●	●	●	●	●	●	●	●
Spectrum Violet	●				●	●	●	●	●						●							
Rose Malmaison	●				●	●	●	●										●				
Alizarin Crimson									●		●	●		●			●			●		
Cadmium Red									●	●										●	●	
Spectrum Red	●			●		●		●							●							
Magenta													●		●			●				
Red Ochre				●					●	●					●	●				●		
Rose Madder		●	●																		●	●
Raw Umber		●							●	●				●					●			
Lamp Black					●		●	●	●	●	●	●		●	●	●		●				
Permanent White	●		●	●	●	●	●	●					●	●	●	●	●	●	●	●	●	●
Gold					●										●			●		●	●	●
Silver													●									

	Cherry Basket Brooch	Rose Basket Brooch	Easter Centrepiece	Father Christmas	Christmas Teddies	Winged Head Cherub	Garlanded Cherub	Orange Tree	Kitchen Dresser	Mr Bear Portrait	Mrs Bear Portrait	Rose Cottage
	•	•						•	•	•	•	•
				•								
			•									
			•	•				•	•			
										•	•	
	•		•				•	•	•			•
		•	•	•		•	•		•			•
			•								•	
								•	•			
											•	
				•								
				•	•		•					
	•											
									•	•	•	•
		•	•			•	•					•
				•						•		
	•			•	•	•		•	•	•	•	•
		•	•	•	•	•	•	•	•	•	•	•
	•					•	•			•	•	
				•								

PROBLEM SOLVING

PROBLEM	SOLUTION
Dough cracks at any stage	• Insufficient or poor kneading. Kneading drives out air from the dough. If the air remains, it expands on baking to crack the dough. • Stray air bubbles can also expand to crack a thick model cooked too quickly at too high a temperature. The aim is to dry out dough slowly, even overnight at a very low temperature. • Mixture too dry. This is usually noticeable during kneading. • Unexplained cracking after baking, often with a loud report. This rarely happens to painted and varnished dough so finish as soon as possible. • A fine craze can occur in paint. This happens to colours mixed with white. Permanent White seems less inclined to craze.
Repairing cracks	• Fill with hard-drying glue. Leave to dry. Use reasonably thick paint to cover the glue. • Fill with soft dough, smooth and bake. Sand down.
Rope splits vertically	• Dough not kneaded properly. Scoop up dough, re-knead and start again.
Discoloured and dented model	• Too liberal use of water when fixing pieces together. Dampen the piece being attached rather than the main model. • Denting caused by dough being too soft.
Blisters on flat model	• Insufficient kneading or too high oven temperature. Check dough after 20 minutes and prick blisters, weigh down and bake.
Baked item will not leave baking sheet. Usually happens to dense models	• Dough not cooked. Run a palette knife under it to release and pierce dough with fine needle from the back: if it goes in easily and comes out smeared, dough is not cooked. Turn model upside down on foil and continue baking until hard.
Model drops off the wall, leaving a rusty hook	• Dough hanging in damp atmosphere or on damp wall softens. Warn clients not to hang dough in humid conditions.

BASKETS AND BOWLS

Fruit Bowl
Weaving strips of dough over an ovenproof bowl.

Bowls are among my favourite projects because they have everything: they are easy to make, look impressive as gifts, and are versatile and useful as well.

The basic technique of weaving dough, either on the inside or the outside of an ovenproof dish, is very simple; however, it is important to choose the dish with care. If you are modelling on the outside of the dish, make sure that it does not have a rim under which the dough can get caught as it expands slightly during baking. On the other hand, if you are weaving dough on the inside of the dish, you will need a rim to support the decoration.

Decorating the dish is the best stage of the modelling. Although I have used flowers and fruit in this book, you might like to experiment with other designs, such as different-shaped breads, shells and fish. Alternatively, you may prefer to concentrate on one type of fruit, such as cherries or strawberries, on any one project.

A basket, such as the Primrose Basket, see page 22, is the first item I demonstrate to beginners because it includes almost all the basic techniques of dough modelling. By the time you have woven and twisted the basket, then made the leaves and flowers you will almost be a fully fledged dough modeller.

· FRUIT BOWL ·

ovenproof bowl, see method
cooking oil
Paste Dough using 20 flour × 20 salt ×
6 paste, see page 8
Golden Egg Glaze, see page 8
leaf cutters: ivy, rose and a very small cutter
black stamens
cloves
primrose cutter

1 You need an ovenproof bowl without a lip or rim. My bowl measured 16.5cm (6½in) in diameter and 10cm (4in) deep but the size may vary slightly according to what is available. Brush the outside of the bowl with oil and invert it on a baking sheet.
2 Using half the dough, make a twist to encircle the now-inverted top of the bowl, see page 9. Arrange this on the sheet, around the bowl and fix the individual ropes of dough together with a little water to avoid having an obvious join in the twist.
3 Roll out the remaining dough to 6mm (¼in) thick and cut ten strips approximately 25 × 2.5cm (10 × 1in) depending upon the exact size of your bowl. Weave the strips over the bowl, see page 9, and leave their ends overhanging the twist on the baking sheet.
4 When the weaving is complete, trim each strip, brush the end with a little water and fix it to the twist. Brush with glaze, then bake at 145°C (290°F/Gas 1½) for about 1 hour. Leave to cool on the baking sheet.
5 Remove the bowl from the mould and stand

Fruit Bowl

19

it the right way up. Knead the scraps and trimmings of dough from making the bowl and divide this in half. Reserve one piece for modelling the fruit and roll out the rest thinly.

6 Cut out eight rose leaves and vein them with the back of a knife. Arrange these in pairs at regular intervals around the rim of the bowl, fixing them in place with a little water.

7 Mould eight small balls from the remaining dough to represent cherries. Cut the thick ends from the stamens and push one into each cherry. Push the rest of the stamens into the opposite side of the cherries to represent stalks. Arrange the cherries in pairs, close to the leaves. Tuck the loose ends of the stamens under the leaves.

8 Mould two or three slightly larger balls of dough into apples and arrange them around the dish. Use the very small leaf cutter to make a leaf for each apple and attach this to the top, with a clove for a stalk.

9 Model similar pieces of dough into pears and place them randomly between the other fruit. Press a clove right into the dough at the base of each pear, leaving just the star-shaped end showing. Push another clove into the top to resemble the stalk.

10 Build up a bunch of grapes on each side of the rim using very small balls of dough. Cut out an ivy leaf and place this at the broad end of the bunch, with a stalk made from a clove.

11 Cut out some primroses and a few leaves to fill in any spaces. Stand the bowl on the baking sheet. Brush the inside with glaze, taking care not to get any glaze on the fruit, leaves or flowers. Bake at 145°C (290°F/Gas 1½) for 1 hour.

Painting and Finishing

● Paint the leaves and fruit as for the Fruit Garland, see page 30. Varnish several times, inside and out, with yacht varnish.

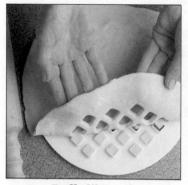

Daffodil Bowl

Using a lattice pie top cutter to make the bowl.

·DAFFODIL BOWL·

Paste Dough using 20 salt × 20 flour ×
6 paste, see page 8
lattice pastry cutter
cooking oil
ovenproof dish with lip
daffodil cutters
cocktail stick (toothpick)

1 Roll out half the dough on a lightly floured board until large enough to cover the lattice pie cutter and about 6mm (¼in) thick.

2 Place the cutter on the board, cutting edge up, and lay the rolled-out dough over it. Roll over the dough lightly until you can see that the lattice has been cut.

3 Oil the dish and line it with the dough lattice, making sure that the lattice pattern is symmetrical. Trim off excess dough draped over the outer edge of the rim.

4 Use half the remaining dough to make a rope long enough to encircle the top of the pie dish, see page 9. Dampen the lattice rim and fix the rope on top, flattening it with your fingers until it is the same width as the lip, starting and finishing at one corner.

5 Roll four fine ropes of dough to represent daffodil stems and fix one of these on each side of the rim. Roll four similar stems each with one end slightly fatter. Model the thick ends into daffodil buds. Fix these in place alongside the first stems.

6 Roll out the rest of the dough. Make four daffodils, see page 14, then arrange them on the plain stems. Cut out eight narrow, pointed leaves, see page 12, and arrange these beside the daffodils, two to each flower. Model a little bird, see page 12, and place him somewhere on the rim among the flowers to complete the decoration. Bake at 145°C (290°F/Gas 1½) for 2 hours.

Daffodil Bowl

Daffodil Bowl continued

Painting and Finishing

● Paint the leaves and stems with a thin mixture of Sap Green. While the bud stalk is still damp, blend a little watery Raw Umber into the bud base before painting most of the rest of the bud in Sap Green, just leaving a 'V' shaped opening at the top for the tip of the flower. Leave to dry.

Paint the petals and the tips of the buds Lemon Yellow. Allow to dry before painting the trumpets Golden Yellow, tipped while still damp with a mixture of Golden Yellow and Rose Madder. Paint the bird Lemon Yellow, then blend some of the Golden Yellow and Rose Madder mix on his chest and wing tips. Varnish inside and out with two or three coats of yacht varnish.

· PRIMROSE BASKET ·

Original Dough using 16 flour × 8 salt,
see page 8
fresh primrose leaf
primrose cutter
modelling tool

1 Roll out half the dough to 6mm (¼in) thick, then cut it into nine 15cm × 12mm (6 × ½in) strips. Working directly on a baking sheet, weave a mat which is four strips high and five strips wide, see page 9. Trim the strips so that the ends of each lay touching the baking sheet.

2 Roll two 15cm (6in) long finger-thick ropes from some of the remaining dough. Lay these vertically along either edge of the woven piece, flatten them, then trim off any excess.

3 Make a twist from two similar ropes, see page 9, and lay this across the bottom of the basket, then trim it to size. Make a 25cm (10in) twist and attach it to either side of the top of the basket to form a handle.

4 Make a third twist, about 20cm (8in) long, and fix this horizontally across the top of the basket, curving it down slightly in the middle so that the lattice shows above it. This twist should conceal the handle joins.

5 Knead all the remaining dough together and roll it out thinly. Cut out about five primrose leaves using the fresh leaves as a guide and to imprint the vein pattern on the dough, see page 12. Arrange these on the basket so that some of them drape over the edge and a couple stand at the back attached to the lattice.

6 Cut out at least 20 primroses and arrange them on the basket. The flowers should overlap each other in some places. Indent the middle of each flower with a modelling tool. Bake at 145°C (290°F/Gas 1½) for about 2½ hours.

Painting and Finishing

● Make a soft watery green by mixing Lemon Yellow and a little white into Olive Green. Paint the primrose leaves with this, making sure that the paint is thin so that the veins show up well. Mix a little white and Lemon Yellow together and paint the flowers. Use the mixed green to paint their centres while the yellow is still fairly damp.

Make an orange colour by adding a little Rose Madder to the Lemon Yellow and use to encircle the green centres when they are quite dry. Varnish once or twice with polyurethane clear gloss varnish.

CRAFT TIP

If you want to make a flower bud, stamp out the primrose flower, then fold it into quarters and set the pointed end into a small oval of dough. Attach a dough stalk.

Primrose Basket

Strawberry Basket

Pressing a lump of dough against a basket to leave the impression of the weave on the dough.

· STRAWBERRY BASKET ·

Original Dough using 16 flour × 8 salt,
see page 8
basket or woven cane object
leaf cutter
cocktail stick (toothpick)
calyx cutter
small primrose cutter
modelling tool
Golden Egg Glaze, see page 8

1 Form a good handful of dough into a ball, then press it firmly against a basket or some other cane object so that the pattern of the weave is imprinted on the dough.

2 Carefully mould the dough into a basket shape without pressing out the impression of the weave. Place it on a baking sheet. Cut a shallow curve out of the dough to form the top of the basket. Make a twist of dough, approximately 12.5cm (5in) long, see page 9, to trim the top edge.

3 Make a slightly thicker, 22.5cm (9in) long twist of dough and fix this in place on either side of the curve in the dough to make a handle. Place a third, thinner 17.5cm (7in) twist across the middle of the basket for decoration. Lastly, make a thin 4cm (1½in) rope and fix it around the bottom of the basket as a base.

4 Roll out half the remaining dough thinly and cut out nine leaves. Vein these with the back of a knife and arrange them in the basket so that some of them are draped over the front of it and over the joins between the handle and basket. Position a few leaves at the back of the basket but do not fix them to the dough until the strawberries are added.

5 Divide the remaining dough in half. Using one portion of the dough, model nine strawberries about the size of small, real fruit.

Use a cocktail stick (toothpick) to mark a strawberry-like texture on the moulded fruit.

6 Roll out the second portion of dough, then use the calyx cutter to stamp out a top for each strawberry and fix to the top of each fruit before arranging the strawberries in the basket. Make sure that some of them are attached to the loose leaves at the back of the basket. Secure the leaves when the fruit are in position.

7 Cut out several small primroses. Arrange them around the strawberries and place a tiny ball of dough in the centre of each, then indent it with a modelling tool.

8 Brush the basket with Golden Egg Glaze, avoiding the parts to be painted and the twists on the basket itself. Bake at 145°C (290°F/Gas 1½) for 2½ hours.

Painting and Finishing

● Paint all the leaves and strawberry tops with Olive Green and the strawberries with Spectrum Red. Mix a little Red Ochre into some Permanent White to make the dusky pink for the flowers, then when they are dry paint their centres with Golden Yellow. Encircle the centres with a mixture of Olive Green and Permanent White. Varnish with polyurethane clear gloss varnish

Strawberry Basket

25

GARLANDS AND WREATHS

Victorian Wreath

Indenting the centres of the flowers as the decoration is built up on the wreath.

In the following designs, I have tried to avoid the rather folksy tradition related to making garlands and wreaths. There is no reason why dough should be limited to rustic subjects, as it so often is, and you will find that it is possible to borrow ideas from a far wider range of artistic traditions and to translate them successfully into dough-modelling techniques. The flower garland on page 30, for example, was inspired by the border on an old porcelain plate, while the fruit garland owes its existence to a Victorian frieze.

Look for inspiration in medieval wood carvings or sculpture, as well as paintings, illustrations, textile designs and so on. You never know – you might move dough modelling out of the kitchen and into the drawing room.

· VICTORIAN WREATH ·

25cm (10in) round plate
Original Dough using 20 flour × 10 salt,
see page 8
large leaf cutter
rose cutters
modelling tool
blossom plunger cutter

1 Using a dinner plate as a template, draw a circle on a baking sheet using a pencil or felt-tip pen.
2 Use slightly more than half the dough to make a rope measuring 75cm (30in) long. Arrange this just inside the circle on the baking tray and join the ends of the dough with a little water to make a ring. Keep the join at the base

of your design. Flatten the rope slightly with your fingers so that it is about 5cm (2in) wide.
3 Roll out approximately two-thirds of the remaining dough and cut out 29 leaves. Use the back of a knife to make veins on the leaves and arrange them on the wreath. Fix four leaves pointing right, four pointing left and one pointing straight down over the join in the wreath. Halfway up on either side of the wreath, fix eight leaves: four pointing up and four pointing down. Set aside the remaining four leaves.
4 Make three roses, see page 13, and place one in the centre of each group of leaves. Make six small roses, omitting the final four petals, and arrange these in pairs on either side of the large roses.
5 Model a large bow, see page 10 extending the ribbons to about 17.5cm (7in). Arrange this at the top of the wreath, curling the ribbons with their ends tucked behind the groups of roses.
6 Arrange the reserved leaves in pairs in the curves of ribbon on either side of the bow. Make two small roses and place on the leaves.
7 Model two little birds, see page 12, and place them facing one another on either side of the base group of roses.
8 To make the sprays of flowers between the birds and roses, roll out four fine ropes, approximately 4cm (1½in) long. Arrange these in pairs to represent stalks, with the ends nearest the roses joined together. Using a sharp knife, cut four elongated leaves from rolled-out dough and arrange them in pairs at the base of the stalks. To make the flowers, build up

Victorian Wreath

several little balls of dough at the tops of the stalks and indent each one with a modelling tool.

9 Cut out about 30 small blossoms and arrange these liberally all over the wreath wherever there is a bare space. Indent the centres of the blossoms with a modelling tool.

10 Use a modelling tool to make two holes behind the bow at the top of the wreath to hang it when finished. Bake at 145°C (290°F/ Gas 1½) for about 3 hours.

Painting and Finishing

● Paint the leaves with patchy, watery Olive Green, leaving occasional uneven patches bare. While still damp, wash some thin Rose Malmaison on the bare patches and blend with a clean damp brush.

Paint the roses individually with thin Permanent White and tip the edges of the petals with some Rose Malmaison while still damp. Gently blend the colour down into the petals with a clean damp brush.

Paint the little birds white. Blend a little Rose Malmaison into their chests and some thin Ultramarine on the tips of their tails and wings.

Mix some Permanent White with some Ultramarine and paint the little blossoms like forget-me-knots, blushing the blue slightly with a little thin Rose Malmaison. Paint the small sprays of flowers white. Mix a little Olive Green into white to paint the leaves and stalks. Dab a little of this pale green into the centre of each flower.

Mix some Spectrum Violet with an equal amount of Permanent White to paint the bow and edge it with Gold when dry. Finally, paint the centres of the forget-me-knots and the birds' beaks with Golden Yellow. When dry, varnish with clear gloss polyurethane varnish.

CRAFT TIP
Holes in garlands are for hanging; hooks are for tying decorative ribbons through.

·FRUIT GARLAND·

Original Dough using 16 flour × 8 salt,
see page 8
leaf cutters
cloves
50cm (20in) net
butterfly cutter
small primrose cutter
modelling tool
hanging hooks, see page 14

1 Take some dough and make two ropes, see page 9, each 30cm (12in) long and tapered slightly at both ends. Wind the ropes together into a twist, see page 9, and curve this slightly as you place it on a baking sheet.

2 Roll out a small piece of dough, then cut out several leaves of various sizes and mark veins on them using the back of a knife. Arrange these at random on the garland, saving a few to fill any spaces later.

3 Make two or three balls of dough for apples and fix them on the garland among the leaves. Push a clove into each apple, star-shaped end first, so that the stalk is left sticking out.

4 Model two or three similar balls, only this time taper one end of each slightly to make a pear shape. Arrange on the garland. Push a clove, stalk end first, into the broad end of each pear. Discard the stars from two or three cloves and push the stalks, cut ends first, into the tops of the pears.

5 Working directly on the garland, build up tiny balls of dough into two or three bunches of grapes. Finish these by adding a clove stalk at the broadest end of each bunch.

6 Cut several pieces of net, each approximately 5cm (2in) square. Place a small ball of dough in the centre of a square of net. Gather up the net around the dough, then

Fruit Garland and Flower Garland, see page 30

Fruit Garland

*Squeezing dough through a small
piece of net to make a blackberry.*

*Carefully use a knife to transfer the
blackberry from the net directly to
the garland.*

CRAFT TIP
The holes in the garland allow
nails to be used to secure it
safely to a wall.

squeeze the dough out through the holes. As
the dough is forced through the net it forms a
blackberry-shaped ball: remove this carefully
by sliding a knife underneath it and transfer it
straight to the twist. Fix the blackberries in
groups of three or four, securing them with a
little water.

7 Mould several balls the size of small cherries
and arrange them in pairs on the twist. Roll
very thin ropes of dough for the stalks and
arrange these on the cherries, joining the stalk
ends of each pair together.

8 Model fairly small oval shapes for plums and
mark a groove down each with the back of a
knife. Arrange these in groups of three.

9 Roll out some dough and cut out a butterfly,
see page 11, then arrange it on the garland.
Stamp out small primroses and use them, with
the reserved leaves, to fill gaps on the garland.
Make sure that you leave a little of the dough
showing through, otherwise the decoration
will look a little cluttered.

10 Use a modelling tool to make a hole 6mm
(¼in) from the edge of the dough at each end
of the garland. Push two hanging hooks into
the ends, then bake the garland at 145°C
(290°F/Gas 1½) for about 2½ hours.

Painting and Finishing

● Paint the apples with watery Linden
Green, then while still damp streak them
gently with equally watery Spectrum Red.
Do not add red all over but keep it more or
less on one side and around the stalk. Blend
these colours together with a clean damp
brush. Treat the pears in the same way using
Golden Yellow instead of Linden Green.

Paint the grapes in pure Spectrum Violet
and add a little Rose Malmaison to this to
paint the plums. Add a little more Rose
Malmaison to get a purple-red which is just
right for painting the cherries.

Paint the blackberries with a brushful of
clear water before adding some thin Lamp
Black. Leave a small irregular patch of the
blackberry unpainted and trickle some
watery Linden Green and Rose Malmaison
on this patch, so that the paint merges with
the black and gives the appearance of under-
ripe fruit. Paint the leaves in a similar way,
using Olive Green as the base coat, and Rose
Malmaison and Golden Yellow for the
patches. Blend these colours with a clean
damp brush.

Paint the flowers a dull dusty pink by
mixing a little white into the cherry mixture.
When they are quite dry, add a centre of
Golden Yellow tipped with a little purple.
Finish by painting the cherry stalks with
Lamp Black and the butterfly in warm
oranges and yellows, made by mixing Rose
Malmaison and Golden Yellow. When dry,
varnish with clear gloss polyurethane varnish.

·*FLOWER GARLAND*·

*Original Dough using 12 flour × 6 salt,
see page 8
leaf cutters
rose cutters
carnation cutters
daffodil cutters
primrose cutters
blossom plunger cutter
wooden skewer
butterfly cutter
black stamens
hanging hooks, see page 14*

1 Roll half the dough into a rope, see
page 9, approximately 15cm (6in) long.
Leave the middle section of the dough, then
extend and taper both ends until the rope
measures about 30cm (12in). Avoid making the

tapered ends too thin by reducing the length slightly if necessary. Curve the rope on a baking sheet and flatten it slightly with your fingers.

2 Roll out some dough, then cut out several leaves in various sizes and use the back of a knife to mark veins on them. Arrange the leaves in pairs at both ends of the curved dough: four leaves on either side is usually enough, with the smallest ones nearer the end, all facing the middle. Arrange four large leaves in the middle, so that they cover the base and point outwards. There should be room for another two pairs of leaves, halfway between the middle set and the leaves placed at the ends of the garland.

3 Make a rose and a carnation, see page 13, and arrange them back to back on the centre group of leaves. Make two smaller roses without the final four petals and tuck them into the sets of end leaves. Make two daffodils, see page 14, and place these on the midway pair of leaves.

4 Make two violets, see page 13, and tuck them into the centre arrangement with the rose and carnation. Cut out several large and small primroses, and small blossoms, then use to fill spaces on the garland. Place a small ball of dough in the centre of each of the larger primroses, then use a skewer to indent this and the centres of the other small flowers.

5 Cut out a butterfly, see page 11, for the top of the garland. Trim two of the black stamens and push them into one end of the butterfly's body to represent antennae. Prop up the wings with small rolls of foil if necessary.

6 Use a skewer to make a hole 6mm (¼in) from the edge of the dough at either end of the garland. Fix two hanging hooks at the extreme ends and bake at 145°C (290°F/Gas 1½) for 2½ hours.

Painting and Finishing

● Paint patchy watery Olive Green on the leaves so that some of the dough is uncovered. While still wet add a touch of Rose Malmaison and blend lightly with a clean damp brush.

Paint the roses with pure Rose Malmaison and add a little Spectrum Violet to the mixture to paint the larger primrose-shaped flowers. Paint the outer petals of the daffodils with pure Lemon Yellow and add a little Permanent White to this mixture to paint the smaller primroses. The trumpets of the daffodils and the centres of the larger primroses are painted with Golden Yellow and edged with a mixture of Golden Yellow and Rose Malmaison.

Paint the carnation with Permanent White and, while still damp, tip the edges with some watery Rose Malmaison so that it bleeds into the white a little. Paint the blossoms with a mixture of Ultramarine and Permanent White, then just touch them with pink so that they resemble forget-me-knots. The violets are painted with pure Spectrum Violet and their stamens painted in pale yellow.

The small primroses have Olive Green centres bordered with Golden Yellow. The butterfly can be any combination of colours, you choose; however, this one is mainly painted with a mixture of Golden Yellow and Rose Malmaison on the wings, tipped with Ultramarine and white. When dry, varnish with clear gloss polyurethane varnish.

CRAFT TIP

The Flower Garland has a list of equipment which looks impressive and expensive but, although helpful, it is not essential. The very small blossoms are difficult to make without cutters but they can be replaced by little flowers made from very small balls of dough, fixed in place, then indented with the end of a modelling tool. All the remaining decoration can be made using a sharp knife, a pair of curved nail scissors and a wooden skewer.

Fruit Wreath

CRAFT TIP
To make hanging holes, simply wobble the end of a sharp modelling tool through the dough until the hole is large enough. Alternatively a far neater hole is made by using a plastic drinking straw to remove a little plug of dough.

·FRUIT WREATH·

10cm (4in) round saucer
Original Dough using 20 flour × 10 salt,
see page 8
modelling tool
large and very small leaf cutters
cloves • small piece of net
calyx cutter
cocktail stick (toothpick)
blossom plunger cutter

1 Using the saucer, draw a circle on a baking sheet. Roll half the dough into a 35cm (14in) rope. Form the rope into a ring on the circle. Join the ends with water, smooth with a modelling tool, then flatten the ring with your fingers to about 4.5cm (1¾in) wide. Make two holes through the dough, opposite the join, for threading ribbon to hang the wreath.

2 Roll out half the remaining dough thinly and cut out 24 large leaves. Mark veins in these and arrange randomly on the ring often overlapping the edge, leaving room for fruit.

3 Following the instructions on page 28, make five apples and five pears and arrange these in pairs evenly around the wreath. Make two pairs of cherries and place these on either side, adding a couple of small leaves to cover the ends of the stalks. Model two or three sets of blackberries and plums and arrange these to balance your design.

4 Arrange a bunch of grapes, see page 28, and a small group of strawberries, see page 24, towards the bottom of the wreath.

5 Finally, cut out a few small flowers and fix them here and there where you think they are necessary. Indent the flower centres with a modelling tool and bake at 145°C (290°F/ Gas 1½) for 3 hours.

Painting and Finishing

● Paint patchy, watery Olive Green on the leaves so that some dough is uncovered. While still wet, paint thin Rose Malmaison over the patches and blend the colours with a clean dry brush.

When the leaves are dry, paint the fruit, see page 30 – first the apples and pears; dry before attempting the plums and grapes. Then paint the cherries and the strawberries, see page 24. Paint the flowers first with Permanent White, then add a little watery Rose Malmaison, before they are quite dry. Blend the colour a little with a clean, dry brush. Finish by painting the blackberries. Varnish with one or two coats of clear gloss polyurethane varnish and add a ribbon bow.

CHARACTERS

I have only included two people in this section, both children; however, the possibilities are, of course, limitless and the basic techniques remain the same regardless of the person you are making.

I have made Victorian bathing belles, a series of London street criers, fishermen, ballet dancers, grandmas and grandpas, and even a complete football team, and I am sure that you will feel equally inspired once you get going.

The animals are good fun, too, but I have not been commissioned to make quite such a broad variety of them. Come to think of it, though, I did make an elephant once and there was that penguin . . .

· VICTORIAN GIRL ·

Original Dough using 6 flour × 3 salt,
see page 8
7.5cm (3in) round fluted cutter
wooden skewer
cocktail sticks (toothpicks)
large and small rose cutters
garlic press or clay gun
fine sieve · hairpin

1 To make the legs, roll out two slim ropes of dough approximately 10cm (4in) long. Gently roll your finger 2cm (¾in) from the ends of each rope, making slight indentations. Dampen these, then push the ends of the dough up to form feet. Fix two very thin ropes around the legs, above the ankles, for boot tops. Trim the leg tops on the slant and place on a baking sheet.

2 Roll out three-quarters of the remaining dough, then cut out a fluted circle and make a frill, see page 11. Cut two short lengths of frill and fix them a little way up the legs to represent the lower edges of long bloomers.

3 To make the body, mould a small handful of dough into an oval shape approximately 5.5 × 3cm (2¼ × 1¼in). Place the body on the baking sheet and fix the tops of the legs to it.

4 Make another frill to represent a petticoat, then lay it across the legs, fixing it in place with a little water, and attach the ends to the sides of the legs. Do not attach the petticoat frill to the waist as this makes the model too bulky.

5 Measure your doll from the body top to just above the lower edge of the petticoat frill. Then roll out some dough and cut a piece almost as long as the measurement, by approximately 17.5cm (7in) wide. Taper one end of the dough so that it is slightly narrower at the top than the bottom. Make two small pleats at the top of the dough, facing each other in the middle. Fix these in place. Use a well-floured rolling pin to roll the top edge flat. This should give the effect of a slightly gathered bodice.

6 Dampen the body edges and the petticoat frill; lay the 'dress' on them, tucking it under the body and side of the frill. Hide the petticoat top but reveal its frill by fluting the dress.

7 Make two slim ropes, slightly thinner than the legs and about 7cm (2¾in) long for arms. Shape hands at one end of each, see page 10, and trim the other ends on the slant. Cut two short, narrow strips of rolled-out dough and fix them around the wrists to

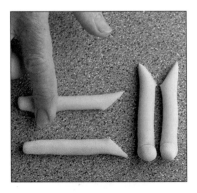

Victorian Girl
*Roll your finger just above the ends
of the legs to shape ankles, then
dampen them and push up the ends
of the dough to shape the feet.*

CRAFT TIP
You can always paint your
doll's clothes in colours you
have available. Try to keep to
my suggestion for the face,
though, and do not be
tempted to buy a tube of
paint labelled 'Flesh Colour'
. . . it won't be!

---

represent cuffs. Attach the arms to the body.
8 Make a miniature doll in a similar way,
about 4cm (1½in) high. Omit details, such as
fingers and petticoat, but mark the eyes and
mouth with a cocktail stick (toothpick) and
add a tiny ball of dough for the nose. Dampen
the back of the doll and lay it in position. Use
the end of a damp brush to lift the girl's hand
and gently bring the whole arm around to
cover the doll. Lift the other hand in the same
way and lay it against her dress, then cover
most of this hand with a small square of dough
to represent a pocket.
9 Fix another wide frill about 4cm (1½in)
above the dress hem to represent a pinafore.
Use a cocktail stick (toothpick) to mark ribbon
holes across the upper edge of the frill. Arrange
two thinner pieces of frill across the shoulders
and meeting at the front. Using the smallest
rose cutter, cut out a circle of dough and cut it
in half, then fix both halves to the top of the
dress to represent a collar.
10 Mould a ball of dough for the head and
mark the eyes and mouth with a cocktail stick
(toothpick). Add a small ball of dough for the
nose. Make the girl's hair by pressing dough
through a garlic press or clay gun. Push some
dough through a fine sieve for the doll's hair,
see page 10.
11 Using a large rose cutter, cut a circle and
attach it to the head for the brim of the hat. Use
a thicker piece of dough to cut a smaller circle
for the crown and attach it to the brim. Trim
the hat with ribbons made from two narrow
strips of dough and a tiny rosebud, see page 13.
12 Make another rosebud and two buttons for
the dress. Make bootlaces from very thin ropes
of dough. Finally push a whole hairpin through
the hat and into the head and body, leaving just
enough protruding to use as a hanging hook.
Bake at 145°C (290°F/Gas 1½) for about
2½ hours.

Painting and Finishing

● Mix some white to a creamy consistency
and thoroughly mix in a very little touch of
Cadmium Yellow. Add a very small amount
of Cadmium Red to make a good flesh
colour: more a creamy beige than pink.
Paint the face and, while it is still wet,
add a little more red and white to some of
the mix and blend in to the cheeks. Paint the
mouth with a slightly darker version of this
and the eyes with a mixture of Ultramarine
and white. Use the rest of the flesh colour to
paint the hands and the arms, and face of the
doll. Use Spectrum Violet and white to mix
the colour for the dress, hat bands and
ribbons. Spectrum Violet is also used for the
stockings and buttons. Paint the pinafore a
mixture of Red Ochre and white. Decorate,
when dry, with a mix of Alizarin Crimson
and white for the flowers and Ultramarine,
Cadmium Yellow and white for the leaves.
Paint the frills and stripes white. A
mixture of Alizarin Crimson and white is
used to tint the roses, doll's cheeks and
pinafore ribbons. Paint the hat and boots
with Raw Umber.
The doll's dress is Cadmium Yellow with
black spots. Add black shoes. Her hair is a
Cadmium Yellow and Cadmium Red mix;
eyes and stockings, Ultramarine and white.

· GEORGE ·

*Original Dough using 6 flour × 3 salt,
see page 8
cocktail stick (toothpick)
old retractable ballpoint pen
medium rose cutter • garlic press*

1 Make legs and feet as for Victorian Girl,
left, making socks instead of boots. Cut

Victorian Girl and George

George
Using tweezers to transfer George's hair from the garlic press to his head.

CRAFT TIP
Painting tartan looks and sounds difficult but it is, in fact, really easy, so have a go.

two pieces of rolled out dough, approximately 5 × 4cm (2 × 1½in). Use a cocktail stick (toothpick) to carefully roll indentations across the wide side, then make these into creases by pressing them together a little. Use the back of a knife to mark the ribbing around the top edge of the socks. Dampen the legs just above the shoes and wrap the socks around them.

2 Cut out two more oblongs of dough 6.5 × 5cm (2½ × 2in) and fit these around the legs to represent trousers. Cut the tops of the legs, including trousers, on the slant and lay together on a baking sheet. Make the body and attach the legs as for Victorian Girl.

3 To make the sweater, cut a piece of rolled-out dough approximately 12.5 × 6.5cm (5 × 2½in). Taper the sides slightly so that the dough fits neatly on the shoulders. Use the back of a knife to mark the ribbing along the bottom edge. Fix the sweater so that it tucks under the body and covers the top of the trousers.

4 Make the arms as for the Victorian Girl and mark ribs on the cuffs. For the skateboard, cut out a long oval about 5 × 2cm (2 × ¾in) and attach four flattened balls of dough for wheels. Indent the centre of each wheel with the old pen. Fix the skateboard against the body. Use a damp brush to pick up the boy's right hand and carefully arrange it over the skateboard. Lay the other hand against the trousers and cover most of it with a small square of dough to represent a pocket.

5 Make the head and hair as for the Victorian Girl. Arrange a narrow strip of dough around the neck to represent a collar.

6 Using the rose cutter, cut out a circle of dough and place it on the head. Press a small ball of dough down over half the circle so that the other half protrudes to represent the peak of the cap. Finish by arranging a fringed strip of dough around the shoulders and down the

front to represent a scarf. Bake at 145°C (290°F/Gas 1½) for about 2½ hours.

Painting and Finishing

● Paint the face, hands and legs as for the Victorian Girl, see page 34, adding a little mud and grime to his knees! Use a mix of Lamp Black and white to make a medium grey for the trousers and socks. Paint the sweater in a mixture of Ultramarine and white. Add the pattern using a fine brush and pure Cadmium Red, Cadmium Yellow and white. The green dots, stripes on socks and Tartan are a mixture of Ultramarine, Cadmium Yellow and white.

The base coat for the tartan is pure Red Ochre. When dry, use a fine brush to draw vertical lines in pure Cadmium Yellow, radiating from the centre of the cap; cross these with horizontal lines in the same colour and allow to dry before painting green lines between the vertical yellow ones. Repeat between the horizontal lines.

Paint the skateboard and the shoes Raw Umber and when dry, mark the lines on the board in red and white, and the laces of the shoes in black and white. Paint the wheels on the board in black with a white circle in the middle of each. Add a couple more red and blue stripes to the socks.

·CATHERINE SHEEP·

Original Dough using 8 flour × 4 salt, see page 8
modelling tool
hanging hook, see page 14
50cm (20in) pale pink ribbon

1 Roll a small piece of dough into four pencil-thin 7.5cm (3in) long ropes, see page 9.
2 Using a sharp knife, make a small cut at

Heathcliff Pig, see page 38, and Catherine Sheep

Catherine Sheep
You need between 60 and 70 coils of dough to build up Catherine's wool.

CRAFT TIP
For a really pig-coloured, luxury pig, give the finished model a good coating of Golden Egg Glaze, see page 8. Then use some watery pink paint and a soft paint brush, to wash a little colour into the glaze on the cheeks, the feet and under the tummy before baking in the usual way.

one end of each rope to represent hooves. Trim the other ends on the slant and fix them together, in pairs, with a little water. Lay the pairs of legs close together on a baking sheet.

3 Knead and mould another piece of dough into an oval shape measuring approximately 8 × 5.5cm (3¼ × 2¼in). Fix this over the tops of the legs, leaving the hooves and legs extending by 4cm (1½in).

4 Take a walnut-sized piece of dough and pinch it into a face shape. Mark the eyes and nostrils with the sharp end of the modelling tool, then fix it to one end of the body. Using the rounded end of the modelling tool, form two very small balls of dough into cup shapes to represent ears and attach them to the head.

5 Roll out several very thin ropes of dough and cut them into 5cm (2in) lengths. Roll each length into a coil: you will need between 60 and 70 coils to make the sheep's wool.

6 Dampen the sheep, then attach the coils in a higgledy-piggledy fashion all over the head and body. Stick a few coils on top of each other to build up the tail.

7 Attach a hanging hook and use the modelling tool to make a hole just behind the head. The hole is to thread a ribbon through when the sheep is finished. Bake at 145°C (290°F/Gas 1½) for approximately 2 hours.

Painting and Finishing

● Use a medium brush to paint the legs and face Lamp Black. Carefully drag some watery white paint over the sheep's coat, so that some of the natural dough colour shows through and gives it some depth.

Add a little speck of Alizarin Crimson to the watery white to paint the ear linings and nostrils. Use a mixture of Ultramarine and white for the eyes. Allow to dry, then varnish. When the varnish is dry, thread the ribbon through the neck hole and tie in a bow.

· HEATHCLIFF PIG ·

The quantity of dough below is sufficient to make two pigs.
Original Dough using 8 flour × 4 salt, see page 8
modelling tool
large briar rose cutter
hanging hook, see page 14

1 Make four legs following steps 1 and 2 as for the Sheep, left. The legs should be slightly thinner than those for the sheep and they should be 5cm (2in) long.

2 Knead a small handful of dough and mould it into a flattened circle of 7.5cm (3in) in diameter. Fix this over the top of the legs leaving 3cm (1¼in) uncovered.

3 For the head, flatten a piece of dough into a 5cm (2in) circle. Fix it in place on the body. Flatten a small ball of dough to approximately 2cm (¾in) across for the snout. Fix it in position, then use the modelling tool to mark the nostrils and eyes.

4 Roll out a small quantity of dough thinly and use the large briar rose cutter to cut out two ears. Attach these in place on the head.

5 Make a thin rope, approximately 7.5cm (3in) long, and attach one end to the pig's rear end. Give the rope a twist, then fix the other end against the body. Fix a hanging hook in the pig's back and bake at 145°C (290°F/Gas 1½) for about 1 hour.

Painting and Finishing

● If you have not already baked the pink colour into the pig, wash some very watery Alizarin Crimson over the tummy, cheeks and feet. Use a medium brush and Lamp Black to paint uneven patches on the pig's sides and ears. Paint the eyes with the same colour. Allow to dry, then varnish.

·*FINLEY FISH*·

*Paste Dough using 6 flour × 6 salt ×
2 paste, see page 8
Fish Template, see page 78
thin card · rose cutters
old retractable ballpoint pen
hanging hook, see page 14*

1 Roll out half the dough to 6mm (¼in) thick. Flour the template, place on the dough and cut around it with a sharp knife. Lay the fish carefully on a baking tray and smooth any rough edges.

2 Roll out the remaining dough thinly. Then, using the small, medium and large rose cutters, cut out an assortment of circles. You need approximately 23 very small; 23 medium; and 17 large circles. Dampen the fish and, starting at the base of the tail, begin arranging circles in overlapping rows. Begin with two rows of small circles, followed by two rows of medium, three rows of large, a further two rows of medium and finally two rows of small circles. This arrangement should take you up to the head of the fish which is left plain.

3 Place a tiny ball of dough in position for an eye and mark the centre with the old ballpoint pen. Join a small, thin rope of dough into a tiny circle for the mouth.

Finley Fish

CRAFT TIP
Add two or three coats of varnish to enhance this model and make it glitter and shine.

4 Use the back of a knife and the retracted pen to decorate the tail fin and head. Fix a hanging hook in position and bake at 145°C (290°F/Gas 1½) for about 1½ hours.

Painting and Finishing

● Make up very thin washes of Magenta, Ultramarine, and Viridian. Mix Magenta and white to make a pale pink, also make a wash of this.

Brush the fish with water. Using a large soft brush, run the pink along the stomach. Do the same with the Magenta wash working a little higher up the body, then use the Ultramarine wash above the Magenta. Finally, wash on the Viridian at the very top and allow the colours to mingle. You can encourage the mingling a little with a clean brush but do not mix the colours too much or they will become muddy.

When the paint is almost dry take some silver paint on a dry brush and drag it across the top scales of the fish so that it lands in uneven patches and catches the light, like real scales. Allow to dry and varnish.

· CLAUDE ·

The quantity of dough makes two cats.
Original Dough using 8 flour × 4 salt,
see page 8
modelling tool · small rose cutter
hanging hook, see page 14

1 Take a small piece of well-kneaded dough and mould it into four 6.5cm (2½in) pencil-thin ropes, see page 9.
2 Flatten one end of each rope slightly, then make four small cuts along the flat edge to represent toes. Round-off each toe with a damp brush. Follow the instructions for Heathcliff Pig, see page 38, to the end of step 3.

3 Flatten two small balls of dough and fix them to the face to make whisker pads. The pads should be touching and they look more realistic if you use a damp brush and a modelling tool to smooth their upper edges into the face. Form a tiny piece of dough into a triangular-shaped nose and fix it in place between the tops of the pads.
4 Roll out a small amount of dough thinly and use the rose cutter to cut out a small circle. Cut this into quarters so that you have four wedges. Use only two wedges: press them out slightly with your fingers and fix them in position for the ears.
5 Cut a thin strip of dough, long enough to fit around the cat's neck. Attach this with a little water before adding a bow, see page 10.
6 Make a 7.5cm (3in) rope for the tail and fix it in place. Attach a hanging hook and bake at 145°C (290°F/Gas 1½) for about 1 hour.

Painting and Finishing

● Mix a little Raw Umber and white together, and paint everything except the bow and the parts that are going to be white. Using Raw Umber, white and Lamp Black, mix a lighter brown, a darker brown and black. Using these three colours alternately, paint tabby markings all over the face and the body, with a striped effect on the legs and tail. Paint the tip of the tail, face, bib and paws white, and, while this is still damp, mix a little Alizarin Crimson and white together, then blend the pink on his whisker pads and toes. The ear linings may also be tinted pink.

Paint the eye shapes Sap Green, then add the pupil and outline in black. The bow is a mixture of Ultramarine and white, spotted with white. I have added a few black dots to the whisker pads but be very delicate with these or they can look a bit grotesque.

Claude and Cat Napping, see page 44

WINDOWS

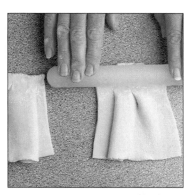

Nursery Window

Make sure that all the pleats are facing towards the middle before rolling the top edge flat.

I have included two styles of windows in this book but if you look around the buildings near your home, or in books, you might be inspired to invent a few more.

The main thing to remember about windows is to decide before you begin whether the clutter on the window sill is meant to be on the inside or the outside. I was once seriously criticised by quite a mature lady because I had modelled a teddy bear on what was obviously an outside window sill, and thereby greatly endangered his life.

On another occasion, I spent a great deal of time modelling a beautiful, rustic window box, full of geraniums and trailing leaves, only to find after I had baked the model that I had also put wonderful billowing curtains (drapes) on the same side . . . so be warned about the possible pitfalls and plan ahead.

·NURSERY WINDOW·

Window Template, see page 78
thin card
Paste Dough using 12 flour × 12 salt ×
6 paste, see page 8
small heart cutter
old retractable ballpoint pen
modelling tool
floristry wire
hanging hooks, see page 14

1 Trace the template, see page 78, then cut it out in thin card. Roll out one-third of the dough to 6mm (¼in) thick, then cut a rectangle of dough measuring 14 × 10cm (5½ × 4in) and place it on a baking sheet. Use the window template to impress the shape of the panes in the dough. Press it down firmly, then lift it off cleanly each time. Use a sharp knife to cut around the indentations. Carefully remove the squares of dough.

2 Make a rope of dough, a little fatter than a finger and 14cm (5½in) long, and flatten it slightly. Dampen the rope and butt it up to the dough under one long edge of the window to form the sill. Decorate the sill with heart indentations, made by gently pressing the cutter into the dough, and dots made with the old pen.

3 Take a generous two-thirds of the remaining dough and roll out thinly. Cut out two curtains (drapes), measuring 15 × 12.5cm (6 × 5in) and one pelmet (valance) measuring 30 × 4cm (12 × 1½in). Pleat each curtain along the top, dampening the pleats to hold them in place and making sure that, on each curtain, they face the middle of the window when in position. Dust the pleats with a little flour, if necessary, to absorb any excess moisture, then carefully roll out their top edge so that they are not too bulky.

4 Wet the top and side edges of the window and fix the curtains (drapes) in place, arranging them as though they are blowing in a breeze. Remember to leave enough room for the bear and the flowers on the window sill. Trim off any excess dough at the top before pleating and fitting the pelmet (valance) using the same technique.

5 Make a teddy bear, see page 12, and place him on the window sill with one paw extended

Nursery Window

Cat Napping
Cutting the scalloped edge for the blind (shade).

to hold a honey jar. Follow the instructions for making pots, step 5 opposite, to make the honey jar. Make the large flower vase by the same method; however, instead of indenting a rim, remove the pot from the modelling tool and carefully mould it into a vase shape by pressing and curving the rim outwards with your fingers.

6 Place the vase on the window sill, then cut out and arrange some leaves in it. Take several small balls of dough and model them into ovals, then flatten them slightly at one end so that they resemble tulips. Cut a short piece of floristry wire, dampen one end and push it into a tulip. Repeat with the remaining flowers, then arrange them in the pot among the leaves.

7 Attach a hanging hook at either end of the top of the window and bake at 145°C (290°F/ Gas 1½) for about 2½ hours.

Painting and Finishing

● The curtains (drapes) are painted with a mixture of Ultramarine and Permanent White. When dry the stripes are painted in Permanent White, with a steady hand!

The bear is painted with Yellow Ochre, with just a blush of watery Red Ochre on his nose and whisker pads.

The pot is also painted in watery Red Ochre and decorated, when dry, with Gold. The bear's bow, hearts and some of the tulips are painted in various combinations of Magenta and white, while other tulips are painted with Spectrum Violet. The leaves are painted in Olive Green and the honey pot is pale pink with black lettering.

·CAT NAPPING·

Window Template, see page 78
thin card
Paste Dough using 6 flour × 6 salt ×
2 paste, see page 8
small heart cutter
cocktail stick (toothpick)
modelling tool
small bird cutter
small leaf cutter
blossom plunger cutter
floristry wire
small rose cutter

1 Trace the window template, see page 78, then cut it out in thin card. Roll out half the dough to approximately 6mm (¼in) thick. Cut out a rectangle measuring 12.5 × 9cm (5 × 3½in), place it on a baking sheet and press the window template down on the dough. Lift off the template to leave the imprint and repeat for all six panes, arranged in pairs. Cut around each imprint and carefully remove the squares of dough.

2 Roll out some dough slightly thinner than above and cut out a rectangle 9 × 6.5cm (3½ × 2½in). Using a sharp knife, carefully scallop one of the longer edges for the bottom edge of the blind (shade). Dampen the plain sides of the dough and fix it in place behind the window frame so that the scalloped edge reaches halfway down. Use the heart cutter and cocktail stick (toothpick) to mark a pattern of hearts and dots on the blind (shade).

3 Roll a small piece of dough into a rope, as thick as a finger and approximately 15cm (6in) long, see page 9. Wet both ends of this and fix it in the shape of an arch across the top of the window. Mould another small rope into a circle to fill the space between the top of the window and the arch. Fix two small balls of dough where the arch joins the window and one where the arch joins the circle. Indent the balls with the end of the modelling tool and decorate the circle in the same way. Roll out a small piece of dough, cut out a bird and fix it in place where the window joins the circle.

4 Make a slightly thicker rope than that used for the arch and flatten it slightly. Wet the top of the dough rope and butt it firmly up against the bottom of the window to make a sill.

5 Mould a small ball of dough into a flower pot, then carefully push the rounded end of the modelling tool in it to hollow it out. While the dough is still on the modelling tool, use the back of a knife to make a slight indentation around the top to form a rim. Carefully remove the modelling tool and make two more pots. Wet the bottom of the pots and arrange them on the window sill.

6 Cut out several leaves and small blossoms from some thinly rolled dough. Mark veins on the leaves using the back of a knife, then arrange them in the pots. Push a short length of curved wire into each pot to represent a stalk. Push the free ends of the wires back against the window frame or against a leaf so that you have a firm base on which to attach the blossom. Form the flower heads at the top of the wires by fixing several small blossoms in a group.

7 Make a small sitting cat, see page 11, and place it on the window sill close to the pots. Fix the hanging hook and bake at 145°C (290°F/ Gas 1½) for about 2 hours.

Painting and Finishing

● Slightly tint some watery Permanent White with a little Alizarin Crimson and paint the blind. While still damp, fill in the hearts with a slightly stronger mix of Alizarin

and white. When dry, add the pale blue dots and border made from Ultramarine and white.

Using pure Sap Green, paint the windowsill and the circles on the arch. Add a little Red Ochre to this mix to make a darker green for the leaves. Paint the pots with fairly watery Red Ochre and the cat with Lamp Black and white. The little bird should also be painted white and decorated with a little pink chest and pale blue wings. The cat's ear linings and whisker pads are painted in the same pink, and his bow is pale blue with white dots. The flowers are Spectrum Red.

CRAFT TIP
Cocktail sticks (toothpicks), which are often used for dough modelling, are sometimes sold in square-topped plastic pots. These pots make wonderful window cutters when empty.

45

DECORATED INITIALS

Decorated dough initials are quite definitely the most popular and acceptable of all the gift ideas in this book. I am sure that this is because everyone, no matter of what age, loves to be given something which has obviously been made especially for them. This is particularly true if the initial is made even more personal by the addition of some detail which is meaningful to the person for whom it is intended.

I have chosen three basic designs which are suitable for any age group, bearing in mind that the figures can be adapted to more adult interpretation if necessary. Most initials should measure at least 15cm (6in) high to allow plenty of room for a figure; however, those with a floral decoration may be made a little smaller if you wish.

TWISTED FLORAL ·INITIAL·

Original Dough using 12 flour × 6 salt,
see page 8
leaf cutters
primrose cutters
blossom plunger cutter
rose cutters • carnation cutters
small heart cutter
hanging hook, see page 14

1 You will need to make twists of various lengths, depending on the letter required. Some people have difficulty working freehand, in which case it is easier to roughly sketch the shape of the letter in pencil on a baking sheet to use as a guide for shaping the dough twist.

2 Deciding on the technique for shaping the angles, such as the point at the bottom of a 'V', can be a problem. With twisted dough, it is generally more successful to curve the dough, rather than cutting and mitring it, which looks best with the rope-type initial. This is illustrated in the top of the 'A', see page 47, but be careful not to make the curve too broad when shaping 'V' as it can result in 'U'.

3 When you have moulded the basic letter to your satisfaction, roll out some dough and cut out some leaves. Mark veins on the leaves using the back of a knife and fix them over any joins in the dough initials, such as where the bar is attached across an 'A'.

4 Roll out more dough and cut out a selection of flowers: primroses, blossom, roses and carnations. Make the roses and carnations in various sizes, see page 13. Arrange the flowers over the leaves. Roll out a small piece of dough and make a butterfly, see page 11. Attach the butterfly to the initial to balance the design. If you find that the butterfly's wings droop, then carefully prop them up with two small rolls of foil which can be removed after baking.

5 Fix a hanging hook in position and bake at 145°C (290°F/Gas 1½) for about 2½ hours.

Painting and Finishing

● Paint the leaves roughly in Olive Green, leaving some small uneven patches of unpainted dough on them. While the green is still wet, paint the patches with a fairly watery mixture of Rose Malmaison, so that it

Twisted Floral Initial with a small nosegay of flowers

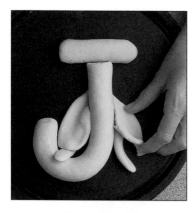

Clown Initial

*Arranging the clown's pantaloons
over his legs.*

Fixing flowers on the initial.

runs slightly into the green. This should give the warm tint of new rose leaves.

Paint the carnation white and while still damp tip the frilly edges of the petals with a little watery Rose Malmaison. Blend the pink into the white, using a clean slightly damp brush, working towards the flower centre. Paint the rose with Rose Malmaison.

Mix a little Ultramarine and white for the forget-me-knots. Add a little pink mixture while still wet and blend the colours so that the flowers are a mixture of pale blue, pink and lavender, where the other two colours meet. The butterfly has a brown body and antennae, made by mixing red, yellow and blue. Add yellow centres to the forget-me-knots and orange ones to the primroses. Mix Rose Malmaison and Lemon Yellow to make orange. Varnish the back and front, several times.

·CLOWN INITIAL·

Clowns are a particularly good choice of decoration for a difficult letter because you can bend them around in all sorts of peculiar poses and they still look realistic.

*Original Dough using 16 flour × 8 salt,
see page 9
equipment for the Victorian Girl omitting
sieve, see page 33
clay gun (optional)
blossom plunger cutter
cocktail stick (toothpick)
garlic press
fine floristry wire
primrose cutter
hanging hooks, see page 14*

1 Follow the instructions for Initial with Figure, see page 50, to mould the chosen initial in ropes of dough.

2 For legs, make two pencil-thin ropes of dough, each 10cm (4in) long. Using your fingertip, gently flatten a 4cm (1½in) end in each rope to represent boots. Place the legs in position on the initial.

3 Mould a pair of arms and hands, making the hands a little larger than usual, see page 10. Fix these in position on the initial in relation to the legs. If your clown is going to hold flowers, make the stems from dough extruded through a clay gun and cut out the flowers using the smallest blossom cutter, then fix them under his hands.

4 For the clown's pantaloons, roll out some dough and cut out two rectangles measuring 6.5 × 4cm (2½ × 1½in). Trim one narrow end of each rectangle in a slight curve, then turn in a narrow hem of dough around the curve and along the long sides. Dampen the legs and lay the pantaloons over them, tucking them under the initial at the waist.

5 Measure the arms and make baggy sleeves as for pantaloons. If the clown's body is beside, or in front of, the initial, make a body following the instructions for Victorian Girl, see page 33. Measure the clown and cut out a romper-suit shape, then turn a narrow hem in the dough on all sides apart from the neck.

6 Make two pieces of frill, see page 11. Carefully dampen the unfrilled edge of each piece and lay one over the other, then fix in place at the clown's neck.

7 Mould a small ball of dough for the head, mark the eyes and mouth with a cocktail stick (toothpick), then make the nose a little larger than usual, see page 33. Fix in place on the frill. Press some dough through a garlic press to make hair. Make a hat as for Victorian Girl. Stick a short length of wire into the hat, then push the opposite end of the wire into the initial. Cut out a medium-sized blossom and use to cover the end of the wire in the initial.

Clown Initial and Initial with Figure, see page 50

Fix a small ball of dough in the middle of the flower.

8 Decorate any joins in the initial with flowers: I have used a primrose cutter to stamp out flowers but you might have other ideas. Fix hanging hooks in the dough and bake at 145°C (290°F/Gas 1½) for about 2½ hours.

Painting and Finishing

● Paint the face as for Victorian Girl, see page 34, omitting the eyes and mouth. When dry, carefully use pure Cadmium Red and a fine brush to paint a wide, curved clown's mouth and a big, fat nose. While this is drying, paint a white oval around one of the eyes and carefully outline the mouth in the same colour. When the white is dry, fill in both the eye holes in Lamp Black and paint a cross on the oval.

Using pure Magenta, paint the clown's suit and dry before painting large white spots. Continue the white on the gloves and the frill. Paint the shoes and hat with Lamp Black and the hair with a mixture of Cadmium Red and Cadmium Yellow.

Use a fine brush and gold to outline all the dots on the clown's suit. You may also edge the frill and make the eyelets for the shoe laces with gold.

Paint the flowers with different mixtures of Magenta and white, and Ultramarine and white. The hat, band, leaves and stems are painted in a mixture of Ultramarine, Cadmium Yellow and white. Finish off the shoelaces and the backs of the gloves in appropriate colours. Varnish, both back and front, several times.

CRAFT TIP
If you only put one hook in an initial it will probably hang at a crooked angle because of the unequal weight distribution. I usually put two hooks in the top and run a ribbon through them. If the initial is destined for a child's room, and particularly for the bedroom door, I also add an anchoring hook at the bottom so that it will outlive the boisterous stage!

·INITIAL WITH FIGURE·

Before you actually start modelling, it is a good idea to make a small sketch of the initial so that you can decide on the best position for the figure. Letters with bars and horizontal lines, such as A, H, B and P, generally look best with the figure arranged over the bar as illustrated, while letters like J, I and L usually look better with the figure leaning against the upright. There are rogue letters, such as K, W and N, but with a bit of jiggling about you will always find somewhere to fit the figure – so don't give up even if you have got a friend called Zaria!

Original Dough using 16 flour × 8 salt,
see page 8
Victorian Girl or boy as for George, see
pages 33 and 34
primrose cutter
stamens
leaf cutters
blossom plunger cutter
heart cutter

1 First draw the initial. Make sure that your dough is particularly well kneaded when you are making this type of initial, especially when shaping a letter with curves, such as B, D or P, as these tend to crack or dent if your dough is either too wet or too dry.

2 With perfectly kneaded dough and your little preparatory sketch to hand, roll out some ropes of dough in suitable lengths for your chosen initial, see page 9. The ropes should be about as wide as two fingers held together.

3 Initials made from ropes of dough always look more professional if the corners are mitred and joins at other angles are cut to fit. However, do not let this prospect frighten you, because, unlike badly mitred wooden corners, mitres in dough can be gently coaxed into perfection using a modelling tool and with a bit of squeezing. Arrange the ropes of dough into the shape of your letter, making sure that all joins are dampened before fixing them together.

4 Following the instructions for either Victorian Girl, see page 33, or George, see page 34, build up the chosen figure on the initial. Decorate with the flowers of your choice. I have used a primrose cutter, added some fluffy stamens at the modelling stage, then painted the flower when baked to represent a dog-rose. I have also added leaves, forget-me-knots and the ubiquitous butterfly, see page 11.

5 When you have completed the arrangement, bake the initial at 145°C (290°F/Gas 1½) for 2½ hours.

Painting and Finishing

● Paint the face, hands, little doll, petticoat and stockings as for Victorian Girl, see page 34.

Paint the dress with a mixture of Red Ochre and white and decorate it with sprigs of flowers and leaves painted in a mixture of Cadmium Red, Ultramarine and white for the flowers, and Cadmium Yellow, Ultramarine and white for the leaves. The hair ribbon is painted using the same mixture as for the flowers.

Paint the leaves on the initial as for those on the dress. The forget-me-knots are painted in pinks and pale blues, made from Red Ochre and white, and Ultramarine and white. Paint the larger flowers white and, while still damp, edge them with a little pink made from Red Ochre and white. Blend in pink with a clean damp brush. Paint the stamens and the centres of the forget-me-knots with a touch of Cadmium Yellow.

Paint the butterfly in any exotic mixture of colours with some white or black spots on the wings, and antennae on the dough in front of the head.

The body and the little girl's shoes are best painted in Raw Umber. Varnish back and front several times.

These little figures are made with small gingerbread cutters. They may be used as brooches or refrigerator magnets.

Initial with Figure
Building up the figure around the initial: adding the petticoat over the bloomers.

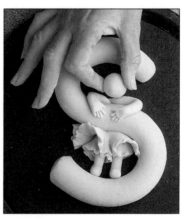

Fixing the head above the arms.

51

DOUGH FOR ALL SEASONS

Love Birds Heart
Making the birds: two birds are cut but only the wings are used from the second shape.

CRAFT TIP
If you want to write a romantic message on the ribbon, use either a very fine brush or a fine waterproof felt-tipped pen.

Dough modelling comes into its own at Christmas when you can use the technique to make a wide variety of gifts and decorations. All the projects in this book make excellent gifts and many of them are easily adapted to a more seasonal mode.

The bowls and baskets, for example, look wonderful trimmed with holly and Christmas roses (made with a primrose cutter). However, my favourite Christmas decoration is the fat flying cherub, and even he can be adapted for Valentine's day by changing his garland to one of hearts and roses.

·LOVE BIRDS HEART·

Original Dough using 16 flour × 8 salt,
see page 8
large bird cutter
old retractable ballpoint pen
leaf cutters · rose cutters
blossom plunger cutter
hanging hook, see page 14

1 Make a fairly substantial twist from slightly more than half the dough, see page 9. Form this into a heart shape on a baking sheet. Mitre the ends of the dough and join them to a point where the heart dips at the top.
2 Roll out some dough to 6mm (¼in) thick and cut out four birds. Neatly cut off the wings from two birds. Notch the ends of these wings and those on the two complete birds to represent feathers. Notch both tails in the same way. Attach the loose wings on top of the wings of the birds, fixing them at a slight angle. Use the back of your knife to make a slight indentation in the beak and the old pen to mark the eyes. Arrange the birds facing each other inside the heart, so that their beaks are just touching and their bodies can be fixed to the sides of the heart. Try to tilt the wings up to fix them to the dip in the heart.
3 Cut four large leaves from some rolled dough and arrange these on either side of the join at the top of the heart. Make one full rose, one smaller rose without the final four petals and one rosebud, see page 13, then arrange these over the leaves to completely cover the join. Cut two smaller leaves and place these back to back on the point of the heart. Roll out some dough to make a thin, large bow with 10cm (4in) trailing ribbons, see page 10. Arrange this under the beaks of the birds with the ends trailing over the edges of the heart.
4 Cut out about 24 small blossoms. Use six to make a posy on the small leaves at the bottom of the heart, then fix the remainder around the roses and ribbon. Fit the hanging hook in the dip of the heart and bake at 145°C (290°F/Gas 1½) for about 2 hours.

Painting and Finishing

● Paint the leaves with watery Olive Green leaving a few random patches bare. While still wet, add a little thin Alizarin Crimson to

Love Birds Heart

53

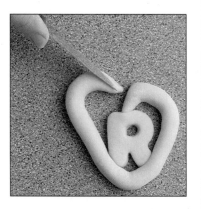

Entwined Hearts

*Cutting the dough to make a neat
join at the top of the heart.*

the patches and blend with a clean damp brush. Paint the roses with pure Alizarin Crimson. Add very little Ultramarine to Permanent White to make a pale blue for the forget-me-knots. Add a little pink, made from Alizarin and white, to the forget-me-knots while the blue is still damp.

Paint the birds with Permanent White and add some pink and blue while still damp. Blend these colours very carefully with a damp clean brush. Paint the ribbon with pale blue and edge with Gold. Decorate the edges of the birds' wings and tails with gold. Use yellow to paint the birds' beaks and mix with Alizarin for the eyes; alternatively, paint both Gold.

· ENTWINED HEARTS ·

*Original Dough using 12 flour × 6 salt,
see page 8
large bird cutter
modelling tool
3 hanging hooks, see page 14
large initial cutters, optional
medium leaf cutter
rose cutters
blossom plunger cutter
small heart cutter
old retractable ballpoint pen*

1 Roll out half the dough to 6mm (¼in) thick. Cut out two birds, then trim the wings off one bird and use to make a bird following the instructions for Love Birds Heart, see page 52. Use the modelling tool to make a hole in the bottom of the bird and fix a hanging hook in the top.
2 Roll out two pencil-thin, 25cm (10in) long ropes of dough and shape these into hearts on a baking sheet. Join the dough in the dip at the top of each heart. Move the hearts so that one

just overlaps the other on one corner.
3 Cut out the chosen initials and fix them inside the hearts. Alternatively, the initials can be made from slightly flattened, thin ropes of dough.
4 Cut out four leaves, mark veins on them, then arrange them in pairs on either side of the joins at the top of the hearts. Place a small rose, see page 13, in the middle of each pair.
5 Cut out several blossoms, arrange three of these on each initial and group the others around the roses. Indent a pattern around the hearts using the heart cutter and old pen, then place a hanging hook in the dip of each heart.
6 Bake at 145°C (290°F/Gas 1½) for 1 hour. Check that the bird is not overbaking and remove it, if necessary, then continue to bake the hearts for a further 30 minutes.

Painting and Finishing

● Paint the leaves with thin Olive Green and the roses with pure Rose Madder. Make a pool of Ultramarine mixed with white and another of Rose Madder mixed with white. Using both thinly, wash the bird in blue adding a gentle blush of pink here and there while the blue is wet.

Thicken the blue slightly and paint the blossoms, adding a touch of pink too. Use pink and blue to paint the heart and dot pattern. Paint a few small green leaves around the blue flowers on the initials. Finish by lining the initials and dots with Gold and by touching the bird's eye, beak, and feathers with a little Gold.

Varnish and allow to dry. Loop satin ribbon through the hole in the bird and the hooks in the hearts. Fix with a stitch of blue cotton or glue.

Entwined Hearts

Mother's Day Dish

*Adding the strip around the rim –
the excess length is coiled and butted
up to the first coil on the corner of
the dish.*

*Attaching the top strip with second
pair of coils and adding the
decorative marks.*

· MOTHER'S DAY DISH ·

ovenproof dish with lip, see method
Paste Dough using 20 flour × 10 salt ×
6 paste, see page 8
cooking oil
old retractable ballpoint pen
rose cutters • leaf cutters
blossom plunger cutter

1 You may use an ovenproof dish of any size providing that it has a rim. I used a dish measuring 24 × 17.5 × 5cm (9½ × 7 × 2in). Brush the inside and rim of the dish with oil and place it on a baking sheet.

2 Roll out two-thirds of the dough to 6mm (¼in) thick, then cut out nine 30 × 2cm (12 × ¾in) strips. Weave the dough strips into a lattice, inside the dish, see page 9, making sure that each strip overlaps the rim lip. Trim the strips to the edge of the dish.

3 Knead any excess dough with trimmings and roll out into a long narrow shape so that you can cut several 2cm (¾in) wide strips. Coil the first 6.5cm (2½in) of one strip and place it on one corner of the dish. Fix the rest of the strip over the woven dough ends around the rim. Add further strips, making neat joins in the dough to cover the weaving all around the rim and to allow a 6.5cm (2½in) length of dough spare. Coil the excess dough in the opposite direction to the first piece, then fix it back-to-back with the existing coil. Repeat once more, making slightly shorter coils of 4cm (1½in) and butting them up to the first coils. Use the old pen to mark a pattern of dots all around the dough rim.

4 Make one large and two small roses, see page 13. Arrange the roses on the corner opposite the coils, with the largest rose in the middle. Cut out four medium leaves, mark veins on them, then arrange them in pairs on

either side of the roses. Place a group of three small blossoms close to the roses on each set of leaves. Bake at 145°C (290°F/Gas 1½) for about 1½ hours.

Painting and Finishing

● Add very little Ultramarine to Permanent White for very pale blue. Using this very thinly, paint the rim of the dish.

Paint patchy, watery Olive Green on the leaves so that some of the dough is uncovered. While still wet, paint thin Rose Madder on the patches and blend with a clean damp brush. Paint the roses and the dots on the lip with Permanent White. While the roses are damp, tip their petal edges with Rose Madder. Blend this towards the centre of each petal with a clean damp brush. Use the pale blue to paint the blossoms and blush with a little Rose Madder. Line both layers of the edge with Gold and continue the lines around the coils on the inside and outside. Encircle each white dot with gold. Varnish inside and outside with two or three coats of yacht varnish.

MOTHER'S DAY
· BROOCHES ·

Original Dough using 8 flour × 4 salt,
see page 8
basket or woven cane object
small leaf cutter
about 12 black stamens
small rose cutter
blossom plunger cutter
brooch fasteners • glue

1 Press a walnut-sized ball of dough against the basket or woven cane object to imprint the pattern on the dough. Place the patterned

Mother's Day Dish and Mother's Day Brooches

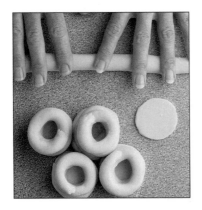

Coiling the rope in layers to make the candle holders.

The coils are assembled in the ring of twisted dough, with the taller one in the middle.

dough on a baking sheet. Roll a very thin, 7.5cm (3in) long twist, see page 9, and fix it in place to form a handle. Roll a very thin, 5cm (2in) long rope and form it into an oval, then butt it up to the bottom of the basket to form the base.

2 Roll out a little of the remaining dough and cut out seven small leaves. Mark the central veins on these with the back of a knife and arrange them over the edge and at the back of the basket. Decorate as below. Bake at 145°C (290°F/Gas 1½) for 1 hour.

CHERRY BASKET

Trim the tops off the stamens, then fix the end of each into a very small ball of dough to make about twelve cherries. Arrange among the leaves, tucking the stamens under the leaves.

FLOWER BASKET

Use the smallest rose cutter to make twelve tiny rosebuds and arrange these among the leaves. Cut out ten of the smallest blossoms and tuck these into any spaces.

Painting and Finishing

● **Cherry Basket** If the baked dough is pale, paint the basket with some watery Yellow Ochre. Paint the leaves with Olive Green. Add a very little of the green to some Magenta to paint the cherries. When dry, carefully paint the cherry stalks with a little black and tint the leaf tips with Gold. Varnish, dry and stick on brooch fasteners. **Rose Basket** Paint the basket and leaves as above, tinting the leaf tips with a little Rose Madder. Paint the roses with Permanent White, adding a slight blush of watery Rose Madder while they are wet. Mix some Ultramarine and white to a pale blue to paint the forget-me-knots, adding just a hint of Rose Madder while damp. When dry, add their yellow centres. Finish as above.

*Original Dough using 20 flour × 10 salt,
see page 8
5cm (2in) round cutter
fresh primrose leaf
nail scissors
primrose cutter
wooden skewer
daffodil cutters
small leaf cutter
blossom plunger cutter • candles*

1 Make a 55cm (22in) twist from one-third of the dough, see page 9. Arrange this in a ring on a baking sheet and join the ends together with a little water.

2 Roll out some dough to 6mm (¼in) thick and cut out seven 5cm (2in) circles. Dampen the edge of one circle. Roll out a pencil-thin rope about 45cm (18in) long, see page 9, and coil it around the edge of the dampened dough circle. Coil the rope up in layers, dampening each layer of rope, to build up a cylindrical candle holder. Complete five more candle holders in the same way, making the last one a little taller by rolling a slightly longer rope. Place the taller candle holder in the middle of the dough ring and fit the others around it, damping them a little where they touch each other and where they touch the outer ring of dough.

3 Roll out some dough slightly thinner than before and press the primrose leaf into it, veined side down. Carefully lift the leaf off the dough and use the nail scissors to cut out the leaf impression in the dough. Make three more leaves and arrange them evenly around the edge of the twisted ring.

4 Cut out 20 primroses and arrange them in groups of five on the twist, close to the leaves. Indent the centre of each flower with the

Easter Centrepiece

wooden skewer. Using the daffodil cutters, model four daffodils directly on the twist, arranging them in pairs on opposite sides of the ring, see page 14.

5 Make six violets, see page 13, and arrange these in groups of three on the ring. Cut out six small leaves and arrange them around the groups of violets. Cut out several small blossoms and fix them around the ring, remembering to fix one to the end of each coil.

6 Finally, flour the end of a candle and wobble it around in each candle holder to ensure that there will be plenty of room for the candles once the ring has been baked. The dough tends to shrink a little during cooking so you may find that you have to shave the ends off your candles before arranging them in the holder. Bake at 145°C (290°F/Gas 1½) for about 3½ hours.

Painting and Finishing

● Make a watery mix of Olive Green and a little Lemon Yellow and wash this over the primrose leaves. Add a little Permanent White to Lemon Yellow to paint the centres of the primroses. When dry, paint the centres with the same green mix as the leaves.

Use pure Golden Yellow for the outer petals of the daffodils and add a little Rose Madder to make the colour for the trumpets. Add a little more Rose Madder and paint the edges of the trumpets while the first coat is still damp. Ring the centres of the primroses with the same colour.

Paint the violets with pure Spectrum Violet and the violet leaves with Olive Green with a touch of Ultramarine added.

Add a little Ultramarine to Permanent White to paint the forget-me-nots. Blush the petals with a touch of Rose Madder and white while still wet.

·FATHER CHRISTMAS·

Original Dough using 12 flour × 6 salt,
see page 8
modelling tool
garlic press
cocktail stick (toothpick)
hanging hook, see page 14

1 Roll two 9cm (3½in) long, finger-thick ropes of dough, see page 9. Roll your finger 2.5cm (1in) from the end of one of them to make a groove. Dampen the groove and push the end up to form a foot. Repeat with the other rope. Trim the other ends on the slant and fix the diagonal cuts together on a baking sheet.

2 Roll out some dough thinly and cut a rectangle measuring 16.5 × 4cm (6½ × 1½in). Make a thin, 16.5cm (6½in) long rope and fix it along one long edge of the rectangle. Make two pleats, facing each other, and close to the middle on the opposite side. Fix the pleats with a little water, then dust them with flour and roll their top edge to make them less bulky. Lay this 'skirt' across the top 2.5cm (1in) of the legs, tucking under each side neatly.

3 For the body, mould a small handful of dough into a smooth egg shape. Wet the back of the dough and arrange it so that 2.5cm (1in) of the lower edge of the 'skirt' protrudes.

4 Cut two 6.5cm × 12mm (2½ × ½in) strips of rolled-out dough and trim the end of one to a point. Overlap the pointed end on the edge of the second strip by 12mm (½in) to make a belt. Fix the belt in position to cover the join between the body and the skirt. Cut a 12mm (½in) square of dough, then cut a smaller square from the middle of this to form a buckle. Place this on the pointed side of the belt, adding a tiny rope of dough to represent

Father Christmas, Christmas Teddy, see page 62, and a holly wreath, see page 63

Father Christmas

Building up Father Christmas and showing the technique used to create the fur texture.

the fastener. Use a modelling tool to make several eyelets in the belt.

5 Roll two 9cm (3½in) long ropes of dough and model hands at one end, see page 10. Trim the other ends diagonally and fix to the shoulders. Make two thin, 5cm (2in) long ropes of dough and arrange around the bottom of the arms as cuffs, then place the hands on the belt.

6 Mould the head in proportion to the body and attach it to the shoulders. Use a small ball of dough for the nose and indent the eyes and mouth with the modelling tool. Flatten two small balls of dough for cheeks and arrange them on the face, then soften their edges with the modelling tool. Push some dough through a garlic press to make a beard and some hair.

7 Make a hat as for the Christmas Teddy, see page 62. Arrange two 7.5cm (3in) ropes of dough on the legs to represent the tops of boots and place two small balls of dough on the coat for buttons. Roughen all the rope trimmings using a cocktail stick (toothpick) to simulate fur. Push a hanging hook into the hat and bake at 145°C (290°F/Gas 1½) for 2 hours.

Painting and Finishing

● Make some flesh colour for the face and hands and paint as for the Victorian Doll, see page 34. Using pure Spectrum Red, paint the trousers, coat and hat but not the fur trimmings. Paint the boots with Lamp Black and the belt with Raw Umber.

Allow to dry thoroughly, then paint all the fur white and the beard, hair, belt-buckle and eyebrows silver.

· CHRISTMAS TEDDIES ·

The quantity of dough below is sufficient to make four teddies.
*Original Dough using 12 flour × 6 salt,
see page 8
teddy bear cutter
cocktail stick (toothpick)
4 hanging hooks, see page 14*

1 Roll out two-thirds of the dough to 6mm (¼in) thick. Cut out four teddies and place them on a baking sheet.

2 Roll out the remaining dough a little thinner and cut out four triangles with 7.5cm (3in) sides to make hats. Wrap one side of a triangle of dough around one head, over one ear. Fold the other two sides under to form a point at the top of the hat and bend this over. Repeat with the remaining hats.

3 Roll eight thin 6.5cm (2½in) long ropes of dough, see page 9, and wrap these around the bears' legs to represent the fur at the top of their boots. Roll four similar ropes, 7.5cm (3in) long and use these to trim the edges of the hats, then add small balls of dough for bobbles. Roughen the bobble and the ropes of dough using a cocktail stick (toothpick) to simulate fur. Attach hanging hooks and bake at 145°C (290°F/Gas 1½) for 1 hour.

Painting and Finishing

● Paint features and boots with Lamp Black and the hats in Spectrum Red. When dry, paint the fur trimmings Permanent White.

Making a small wreath for the Christmas tree. This is modelled from a simple twist of dough, see page 9, made to 20cm (8in) in length. Arrange holly leaves and berries over the join in the dough and fit a hanging hook behind the leaves. Paint with glaze, avoiding the leaves and berries, then sprinkle with poppy seeds. Bake at 145°C (290°F/ Gas 1½) for 1½ hours. Paint the leaves and berries, varnish and add a bow.

WINGED HEAD ·CHERUB·

Original Dough using 16 flour × 8 salt, see page 8
leaf cutters
modelling tool • garlic press
hanging hook, see page 14

1 Make a 17.5cm (7in) rope from a quarter of the dough, see page 9. Taper the ends and flatten the rope with a rolling pin, then tilt the tapered ends up slightly on a baking sheet.

2 Roll out the remaining dough and cut out several leaves in all sizes. Mark veins on the leaves using the back of a knife and arrange them on the rope, overlapping each other with the smallest leaves at the tapered ends and the largest ones towards the middle. Leave a space about 4cm (1½in) across in the centre and towards the base of the rope.

3 Mould a large, slightly flattened ball of dough for the head and place it in the space on the rope. Tuck two large leaves under the head on either side of the chin. Lay two medium leaves on top, then add two very small leaves on top of those.

4 Mould a small ball of dough for the nose and place it in the middle of the face. Mark the mouth with the end of the modelling tool. Arrange two small, flattened balls of dough on the face for cheeks. Smooth the cheek edges with the modelling tool and a damp brush.

5 Push several short lengths of dough through a garlic press to represent hair. Fix a hanging hook in the dough and bake at 145°C (290°F/ Gas 1½) for about 2 hours.

Painting and Finishing

● Leave the dough natural adding a little watery Rose Madder to the cheeks, mouth and chin. Paint two Permanent White

CRAFT TIP
If you want a rosy cherub, like the one illustrated, give the dough a coating of Golden Egg Glaze, see page 8, before baking and tint the cheeks, knees and feet with some watery pink paint while the glaze is still wet.

Garlanded Cherub

Position of wings and legs for the cherub.

Blending the knees into the legs.

lozenge shapes for eyes, remembering to paint the left one first if you are right handed and vice versa. While this is drying, paint the wings white. Make pale blue by mixing Ultramarine and white, and some pink by adding a little Rose Madder to white. Tip all the feathers with a little of each while the white is still damp. Use the pale blue to paint an iris in each eye. When the wings are quite dry edge the feathers with Gold and paint the hair with the same colour. Finish by putting a black dot in the centre of the iris and by outlining the eyes and the eyebrows.

· GARLANDED CHERUB ·

*Original Dough using 8 flour × 4 salt,
see page 8
Wing Template, see page 78
thin card
modelling tool
small holly leaf cutter
blossom plunger cutter*

1 For the legs, roll two finger-thick ropes each about 6.5cm (2½in) long, from a small handful of dough, see page 9. Trim one end of each rope diagonally and fix the two diagonal cuts side-by-side, shortest sides inwards on a baking sheet. Trim feet-ends on the slant, with the longest sides together in the middle. Make four small cuts into the trimmed edges to represent toes, then fix a small flattened ball of dough halfway up each leg to represent knees.
2 Trace the wing template, then cut it out in thin card. Roll out one-third of the remaining dough and press the template down on it to leave a clear impression when removed. Carefully cut around the imprint, then transfer the wings to the baking sheet, above the legs.
3 Dampen the wings and leg tops. Mould a

piece of dough into the shape of a large smooth egg and press this down on the wings and the tops of the legs to represent the body. Mark a belly button using the modelling tool.
4 Roll two pencil-thin, 7.5cm (3in) long ropes of dough and flatten one end of each to make hands, see page 10. Trim the other end of the dough diagonally and fix to the shoulders. Dampen the inside of the hands and lay these on the body.
5 Mould a ball of dough for the head in proportion to the body and mark a smiling mouth using the modelling tool. Flatten a small ball of dough on either side of the mouth to represent cheeks and add a very small ball of dough for a nose. Mark the eyes with the modelling tool. Fix the head on the body and wings, then decorate with small coils of dough to represent hair.
6 Make the garland with small holly leaves and blossoms, adding a few very small balls of dough for holly berries. Fix a hanging hook on the side so that the cherub appears to be flying when he is hung up. Bake at 145°C (290°F/Gas 1½) for about 1 hour.

Painting and Finishing

● If you did not make your cherub rosy before baking, take some very watery Rose Madder and add a little wash to the cheeks, mouth, toes and knees.

Paint the holly leaves with thin Olive Green and the berries with Spectrum Red. Use Permanent White to paint the wings and add a little pale blue, made by mixing Ultramarine and white, to the edges while still wet. Edge the blue with a Rose Madder and white mix, then finish by just tipping the edges with a little Gold and adding a few decorative gold dots. Paint the hair Gold. Paint the little blossoms white, adding pale green in the centre.

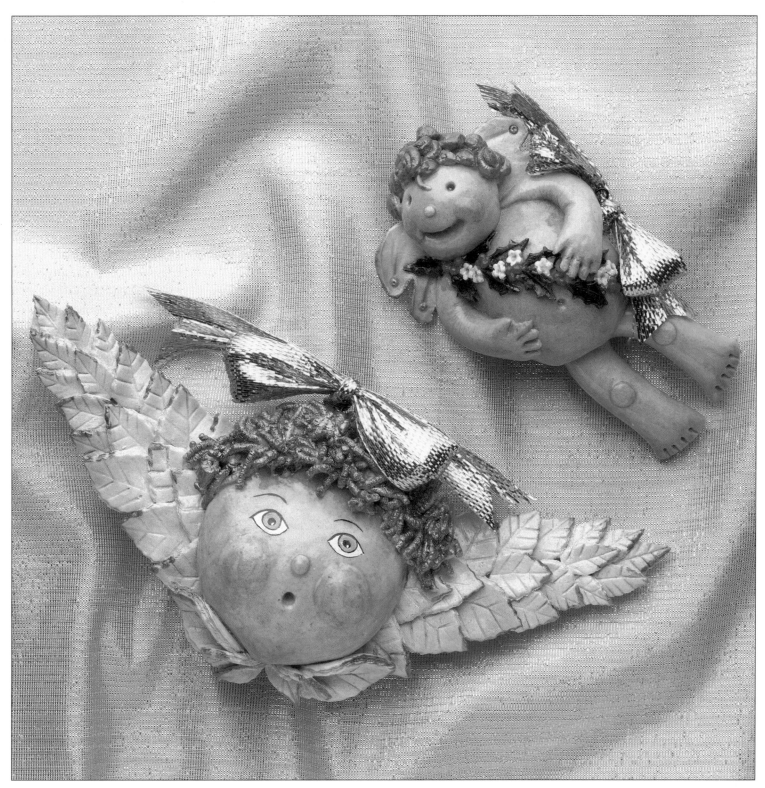

Winged Head Cherub, see page 63, and Garlanded Cherub

65

INDIVIDUAL DESIGNS

Orange Tree

The trunk ready for making the orange tree.

Although it seems likely that some kind of rudimentary dough shaping was around in ancient times, serious dough modelling as we know it today has a relatively short history. Even so, the baskets, bowls, garlands and wreaths included in previous chapters may be considered as traditional subjects within the craft and the tree, which I have included in this section, falls into a similar category.

I decided to illustrate an orange tree, because it really does fruit and flower at the same time; however, you may like to attempt a different theme along the same lines, such as a partridge in a pear tree.

The Bear Portraits and the dresser are not as traditional but they are also very adaptable. What about turning the dresser into a nursery cupboard with toys on the shelves and spilling out of the drawers? The portraits can, of course, be of people, mice or cats, so be adventurous to see what you can invent.

·ORANGE TREE·

Original Dough using 12 flour × 6 salt,
see page 8
medium leaf cutter
blossom plunger cutter · cloves
hanging hook, see page 14

1 Roll about one-third of the dough into a thick, 12.5cm (5in) long rope. Place the rope on a baking sheet and flatten it slightly. Make a 5cm (2in) cut down from the top of the rope to divide it in half, then ease both halves apart a little to make a fork in the trunk. Make several vertical indentations for texture.

2 Roll out two-thirds of the remaining dough and cut out about 40 leaves, then mark veins on these using the back of a knife. Arrange the leaves on either fork of the trunk, gradually working towards the middle until the leaves have joined over the gap. Continue to add leaves, working outwards to create a rounded tree shape.

3 Stamp out about 20 small blossoms and fix these in groups and singly all over the leaves.

4 Mould about eight small balls of dough to represent oranges and push a clove, stalk first, into each of them. Arrange these among the blossoms on the tree.

5 Make a small bird, see page 12, and fix it in an appropriate space on the tree. Push the hanging hook in carefully, making sure that it has a good hold among the leaves. Bake at 145°C (290°F/Gas 1½) for about 2 hours.

Painting and Finishing

● I usually leave the trunk unpainted but, if your dough looks particularly pale, give it a light wash of Yellow Ochre. Paint the leaves Olive Green. When dry, highlight the veins with a little Lamp Black on some leaves and pale Green, made by adding a little white to the Olive Green, on others.

Mix Golden Yellow and Rose Malmaison for the oranges and paint the flowers with Permanent White with a dot of the orange in the centre. Mix a little white into Golden Yellow for the bird and, while still damp, blend a little orange into his chest and the tips of his wings and tail.

Orange Tree

·KITCHEN DRESSER·

Paste Dough using 8 flour × 8 salt ×
4 paste, see page 8
small heart cutter
modelling tool · rose cutters
4 cloves · small leaf cutter
floristry wire · daisy cutter
2 hanging hooks, see page 14

1 Roll out one-third of the dough to 9mm (³/₈in) thick. Cut a rectangle measuring 14 × 9cm (5½ × 3½in) and lay it on a baking sheet. Roll some more dough to 6mm (¼in) thick and cut out a smaller rectangle measuring 9 × 4cm (3½ × 1½in).

2 Dampen the back of the smaller dough rectangle and lay it across the bottom of the first rectangle in position for the drawers. Use the back of a knife to indent the outline of drawers fairly deeply, then decorate them by indenting them with the small heart cutter. Fix a small ball of dough on each for a handle.

3 Roll out some more dough to 6mm (¼in) thick and cut out three shelves measuring 7.5cm × 6mm (3 × ¼in). Cut two 10cm × 9mm (4 × ³/₈in) strips, one 9cm × 12mm (3½ × ½in) strip and one 9 × 1.5cm (3½ × ¾in) strip. Arrange the three shelves evenly along the back of the dresser so that the bottom shelf is 2.5cm (1in) above the drawers and the top one is a similar distance below the dresser top.

4 Fix the pair of cut strips vertically along the sides of the shelves. Make several small, decorative indentations along the edges of these strips with a modelling tool.

5 Fix the 1.5cm (¾in) wide strip across the top of the dresser, parallel with the shelves. Cut three heart shapes evenly across the remaining strip and mark it with decorative indentations as before. Fix this across the top of the dresser. Place two small balls of dough at the bottom of the dresser for feet.

6 To make the plates, use the medium rose cutter to cut five circles of dough. Press the middles in slightly with your finger. Arrange one plate on the bottom shelf and four on the next one up. Make four saucers in the same way using the smallest rose cutter. Place these on the shelf above the plates

7 Discard the star-shaped ends off four cloves, then push the remaining stalks a little way into the edge of the top shelf to represent hooks. Make four very fine ropes of dough each about 12mm (½in) long and curve one of these over each of the clove stalks to represent cup handles. Make the cups by using the rounded end of the modelling tool to hollow out four small balls of dough. Dampen the outsides of the cups and carefully butt them up to the handles.

8 Make three bowls of different sizes as for the cups. Place the largest on top of the dresser, the smallest on the top shelf and the medium bowl on the bottom shelf, next to the single plate.

9 Make a cat, see page 11, and sit him next to the medium bowl. Fill this bowl with little balls of dough to represent oranges.

10 Roll out some dough thinly and cut out several small leaves. Arrange these in the bowl on top of the dresser and push a 4cm (1½in) length of bent floristry wire into the centre. Cut out a daisy and attach this to the end of the wire with a dab of water. Arrange a small ball of dough in the centre of the daisy.

11 Fix two hanging hooks in either side of the top of the dresser and bake at 145°C (290°F/Gas 1½) for about 3 hours.

Painting and Finishing

● Mix a little Yellow Ochre into Olive Green and water it down quite a bit to get just the right colour for this old dresser. The

Kitchen Dresser

Bear Portraits
Adding the whisker pads.

hearts and the lining on the dresser are painted Red Ochre dulled with just a touch of Olive Green.

All the china is painted with Permanent White and decorated with a pale blue rim made from Ultramarine and white. The roses are painted with a mixture of Rose Malmaison and white and the leaves on the plates, and in the big bowl, are painted with Olive Green.

The oranges and the daisy are both painted with a mixture of Golden Yellow and Rose Malmaison. Use some Lamp Black and Permanent White on the cat, with just a little blush of watery Rose Malmaison in his ears and on his whisker pads.

·*BEAR PORTRAITS*·

Paste Dough using 8 flour × 8 salt ×
4 paste, see page 8
medium and small rose cutters
modelling tool
old retractable ballpoint pen

1 Roll out a quarter of the dough medium thick, cut out a rectangle measuring 7.5 × 6.5cm (3 × 2½in) and lay it on a baking sheet. Take a smooth walnut-sized ball of dough and mould one side into an oval for the bear's nose. Dampen the other side of the dough and fix it in the middle of the rectangle. Flatten two small balls of dough and place them side by side on the extreme point of the oval to make whisker pads. Fix a very small triangle of dough, point downwards, at the top of the pads for a nose.

2 Mould a small piece of dough into a rough semi-circle about 6.5cm (2½in) wide by about 4cm (1½in) deep. Arrange this on the rectangle, under the head so that the curved side forms shoulders. Trim off any excess.

MR BEAR

3 Cut two oblongs of rolled-out dough 2.5 × 12mm (1 × ½in). Fix them on either side of the bear's neck, turning the front upper corners back to form a winged collar. Drape a very small, thin square of dough in the opening of his collar and down his chest to represent a cravat. Place a very small ball of dough on this for a tie-pin.

4 For jacket lapels, cut two oblongs of rolled-out dough measuring 4cm × 12mm (1½ × ½in). Notch these, halfway along the long side and fix them in position.

5 Use the medium rose cutter to cut out a circle for the hat brim. Add a small ball of dough for the crown and place the hat on top of the bear's head. Mould two small balls of dough and using the rounded end of the modelling tool, flatten them into saucer-shaped ears. Arrange these on either side of the hat so that they curl the rim up slightly. Follow steps 9–12 to finish and bake.

MRS BEAR

6 Follow steps 1 and 2. Make a 5cm (2in) frill, see page 11, and arrange it around the neck. Make two more frills, 4cm (1½in) long and arrange them over the shoulders, almost meeting in the middle.

7 Make two ears, following step 5, and fix these to the head. Cut a small circle for the hat brim and arrange this at a slight angle over one ear. Use a small rose cutter and a slightly thicker piece of dough to make the crown and fix it on the brim with a little water. Cut two small strips for ribbons and arrange them at the back of the hat.

8 Make two small rose buds, see page 13, then fix one in the hat and one at Mrs Bear's throat.

9 Make two pencil-thin ropes of dough, see page 8, each about 30cm (12in) long. Dampen the edges of the rectangle and encircle it with one rope, joining the ends on a corner and smoothing the join with the modelling tool.

10 Coil the second rope from both ends so that both coils meet in the middle. Fix the coils in this position with a little water, then attach the double coil to the bottom of the frame, with the coils downwards. Mould a 7.5cm (3in) length of rope into a circle and fix this in the middle of the top of the frame.

11 Mould two 7.5cm (3in) ropes and make a single coil at both ends of each rope. Arrange these around the circle so that two coils meet back to back at the top of the circle and the remaining coils are attached to the frame.

12 Mark a pattern in all the ropes using the old pen. Bake at 145°C (290°F/Gas 1½) for 2 hours.

Painting and Finishing

Mr Bear Carefully wash some very watery Red Ochre over the background. When dry, add thin white stripes – or even floral wallpaper – keeping the colours very transparent or they will detract from the portrait.

Paint the face with thin Yellow Ochre, adding just a blush of Red Ochre to the cheeks. Paint the shirt and collar white and make two white almond shapes for eyes. Paint the left eye first if you are right handed so that your hand does not get in the way when you are trying to match the eyes. Reverse the process, of course, if you are left handed.

Use some pure Raw Umber to paint the hat and the base coat for the jacket. When dry, add a little white to the umber and use a very fine brush to paint the herring bone design. The cravat is painted with Permanent Green Middle and spotted with white.

Bear Portraits

71

Take a very fine brush and paint the inverted 'V' between the whisker pads with Raw Umber. Use the same colour to paint the irises in the eyes. Outline the eyes and paint his nose and whisker dots in Lamp Black. Black may be used for the shirt stripes but blue looks better.

Paint the frame first with a good creamy mixture of Red Ochre, then, when dry, take some Gold on a dry brush and drag it over the red. Leave as much of the red showing through as you like to make the frame look more distressed, like an old gilded frame.

Mrs Bear Paint the background and the face as for Mr Bear, except, perhaps, adding a slightly more feminine blush around her nose and in her ears. Paint the roses and frills with Permanent White and tint the edges of the roses slightly with thin Alizarin Crimson.

The dress is a mixture of Spectrum Violet and white, decorated with pure Spectrum Violet flowers. I have used the fatal-sounding Permanent Green Middle to paint the ribbons on the hat and the centres of the flowers. The rest of the hat and the frame are painted with Red Ochre, and the frame is finished with Gold.

CRAFT TIP
The frames may be painted with Viridian as a base coat, then silver may be dragged over the top instead of gold.

· ROSE COTTAGE ·

Cottage Template, see page 78
Window Template, see page 78
thin card
Paste Dough using 12 salt × 12 flour × 6 paste, see page 8
heart cutters
rose cutters
primrose cutter
clay gun
old retractable ballpoint pen
blossom plunger cutter

1 Trace the templates, then cut them out in thin card. Roll out half the dough to 6mm (¼in) thick. Press the cottage template on the dough so that it leaves an imprint when lifted, then cut around this and place the dough cottage on a baking sheet.
2 Use the window template in the same way, to make two upstairs windows and one downstairs window, making sure that you leave sufficient room for the shutters on either side of each window. Lift out the squares of dough from the centre of each window and cut each square in half to make shutters. Stamp out a heart shape in each half. Wet the backs of the shutters and fix them on either side of the windows. Indicate that the shutters are slatted by indenting them vertically with the back of a knife.
3 Roll out some dough thinly and use the largest rose cutter to cut out about 30 circles. Dampen the roof area, then overlap the circles in three rows to represent tiles, starting with the bottom row. Dampen the circles as you place them on the cottage. Model a small piece of dough into a 4cm × 12mm (1½ × ½in) oblong. Use the back of a knife to indent a rim at the top, then tuck this chimney behind the end tiles.

Rose Cottage

4 Cut out a triangle with 6.6cm (2½in) sides. Use the primrose cutter to cut a flower shape from the middle of this, then fix it to the roof with the base level with the bottom row of tiles so that it looks like a gable. To decorate the edge of the gable and the ridge of the roof, use the clay gun fitted with the disc with the largest hole and extrude the dough in loops along the ridge and straight around the gable. Finish by indenting the edging with the point of the old pen.

5 Using the back of a knife, indent a slatted door measuring 5 × 3cm (2 × 1¼in) in the dough next to the downstairs window. Finish the door with a tiny ball of dough for a handle. To make the porch, cut a triangle with 4cm (1½in) sides. Fix this in position over the door, wedging a small ball of dough underneath it to make it bulge out slightly. Using the smallest rose cutter, cut out eleven circles and arrange ten of these overlapping on the porch for tiles. Place the extra circle beside the door for the house number.

6 Make a 15cm (6in) rope, slightly fatter than a finger, see page 9, and butt this up against the bottom of the cottage, flattening it out slightly at the same time. Place a small ball of dough on one end of the rope to represent a tub. Cut six 1.5cm × 6mm (¾ × ¼in) strips of rolled-out dough and fix them vertically on the ball of dough to form the panels. Flatten a thin rope of dough to make the band around the tub and mark nails in it using the point of an old pen.

7 Roll an irregular rope of dough which tapers out at one end and arrange it so that the thick end appears to be growing out of the tub and the tapered end drapes over the porch. Cut some tiny leaves, freehand, out of thinly rolled dough and arrange them along the length of the rose tree. Make several small rosebuds, see page 13, and dot these among the leaves.

8 Make a cat, see page 11, to sit in front of the door. Fit the sieve-like disc in the clay gun and extrude some fine strands of dough. Fix these along the front of the cottage for grass and stems in a flower border. Arrange small blossoms among the grass. The hollyhock, at the side of the cottage, is made by building up a spike of tiny balls of dough and indenting each with the point of the pen.

9 Push a hanging hook into either side of the roof and bake at 145°C (290°F/Gas 1½) for 2½ hours.

Painting and Finishing

● Wash some very watery Red Ochre over the tiles of the roof and porch. While still wet, blend patches of Olive Green on the tiles. Use the same green to paint the tub, then mix it a little thicker to paint the grass and leaves.

Mix some Ultramarine and white to paint the shutters, the edge of the flower-shaped window and the house number plate. Use a mixture of Red Orchre and Yellow Ochre for the cat, adding some white markings. Paint his eyes, the door knob and the rim around the tub with Lamp Black.

Mix a little Rose Madder and white to paint the roses and some of the other flowers. Finish the flowers in various mixtures of reds, pinks and white. Finally, paint in the house number in black. Add a little Red Ochre to the black to paint the earth in the tub and the trunk of the rose tree.

CRAFT TIP
If you do not own a clay gun, the decoration to the roof and gable can be made with a very thin rope of dough, while the finer flower stems and grass may be extruded through a garlic press.

Marketing and Selling

By the time you reach this part of the book, you will probably be addicted to dough modelling. You will know that this is true when your house and those of friends and relatives bear more than ample evidence of your modelling activities and you find yourself resenting all family meals which have to be cooked in the oven.

You are probably searching frantically for other outlets for dough, both to justify and satisfy your craving for making it, while still retaining the goodwill of friends and family who can only take a certain amount of that kind of thing. The solution, I am happy to say, is simply to sell your work to absolute strangers.

There are several ways of selling your craft, each demanding a different degree of commitment and professionalism. So, before you launch your sales campaign you should consider the options and make a few decisions.

EARNING A LIVING OR MAKING EXTRA CASH

- First decide whether you are looking to earn a living by dough modelling or simply wanting to make some pin-money.
- How much time are you prepared and able to devote to modelling?
- Would the family support your venture?
- Don't forget that it is important to take professional advice on book keeping, tax and car insurance.

SELLING OPTIONS

When you have seriously considered the above points, you will be in a better position to decide how to sell your dough.
- Supply family and friends.
- Take a stall occasionally at a bazaar or fête.
- Sell through shops.
- Set up a party-plan selling scheme.
- Sell through craft fairs.

PRACTICALITIES OF MANUFACTURING AND SELLING

These are the points to clearly define before you attempt to sell dough in any quantity and by any means.

The Range Work out which are your most popular pieces before you start your career as a travelling salesman. This is very important before showing your product. Remember that a shop will want confirmation that the range will stay the same for at least a year and, generally speaking, your price should also remain consistent for at least a year. You can always sneak a seasonal piece or two into the range in addition to the basic items.

Price You must work out a price which is acceptable to you and to the customer. Shop owners have high overheads and it is not fair to expect a shop to pay your normal retail price if you run a party-plan scheme in the area or regularly attend craft fairs, so be prepared to give a shop some discount or you will find that you lose their custom. Many craft workers feel exploited by shop owners and what they consider to be very high mark-ups but if the initial price for the work seemed fair and acceptable, the retail price is entirely up to the shop keeper.

Tot up the cost of flour, salt, paint, varnish, travelling expenses and fuel for baking. If you add on what you consider to be an acceptable hourly rate you can make the product unrealistically expensive. The hard costs must be balanced against non-financial factors such as being your own boss and the luxury of having a fulfilling and flexible lifestyle. Provided that you are neither unduly modest nor arrogant, you should be able to price your work within the average range.

Delivery Dates If anyone decides to give you an order, the first thing he or she will want to clarify is the delivery date. Give yourself a realistic time to complete the order and make sure you always keep to it. Do not be tempted to deliver individual items or groups as they are completed as this wastes time, looks very unprofessional and you probably will not get your money any quicker anyway. Shop owners are likely to want to know if you are prepared to make special orders for customers, so have your answer ready, plus expected delivery times for specials and any extra costs you may wish to charge.

Repeat Orders Make templates of even your most simple designs, especially when making for shops, as customers tend to be finicky about any slight deviation from the norm or from the samples on which they based an order. Make a note of colours as well.

Payment Make a clear set of rules for payment and stick to them – this includes special orders, party-plan selling and selling to shops. Goods should be paid for in full when they are delivered. You may decide to ask for a deposit with special orders or with party-plan selling. The nice part of selling to small shops is that you can insist on cash on delivery because the person who takes the order is usually the owner and the cheque signer too. If this is not the case, telephone a few days in advance of making delivery so that staff know the amount owing and can get the owner organised in time to leave payment for your arrival.

Sale or Return I am not keen on leaving goods on a sale or return basis and neither should you be. If a shop owner is not willing to speculate on a small amount of your dough, then you should take it to someone else who will. If your work is any good someone will be prepared to buy some or you can take it to a craft fair.

Do not be taken in by a shop owner who tries to give you the impression that he or she is doing you a favour by displaying some of your work – it can only bring him or her profit and you could very well lose. Work left on a sale or return basis is often poorly displayed because it has to compete for space with goods which have already been purchased. Your dough can quite literally kick around the shop, deteriorating all the time and becoming less attractive until you eventually have to take it home and throw it away. I cannot see why you or I should finance someone else's business.

SELLING TO FAMILY AND FRIENDS

Initially, the worst aspect of this is the embarrassment of charging and stating your price, particularly if you have been free with your favours previously. Adding up the cost of materials, such as flour, paint, varnish and so on, works wonders for personal business acumen though and it is sure to cure your blushes. At first, you may decide to base the price of your models solely on the cost of the materials; however, if your work is still in demand at this basic cost, you ought to consider

something really radical and charge for your time as well!

BAZAARS AND FETES

Generally, this has more to do with self esteem than making money, as these are primarily fund-raising events and you will be expected to contribute part of, if not all, your profit to the cause. It might be worth finding local events, like village fairs, where you are asked to pay a fixed stall fee, then all takings are your own at the end of the day. However, you will have to keep your prices fairly low as many fête-going customers hold very strict views on price control no matter how good the product.

Nevertheless, a bazaar can provide a good setting for your début, particularly if you feel nervous or uncertain about your dough. The feedback from customers will doubtless boost your confidence and their comments can prove more valuable than financial gain at this stage.

SELLING TO SHOPS

The hardest part is actually forcing yourself and your samples through the door – once you have done that, the rest is easy. Most owners run their own craft shops so you will usually find someone behind the counter who can make a decision and give you an order there and then if they like your work.

There are two ways of selling. If you telephone a shop, the chances are the owner has seen a lot of bad work and it is only too easy to put yours into the same category. The excuses for not seeing you are numerous: 'business is bad at the moment, we've tried that before and it didn't sell, we already have a supplier, it's not our kind of thing,' and so on.

It can be difficult to describe dough in glowing terms on the telephone to someone who has never come across it

before. For this reason it is often a good idea to present yourself, unannounced, in a shop rather than opting for the more conventional – and polite – way of making an appointment first.

Prepare beforehand and present yourself and your work in an appealing and organised fashion. Avoid calling at very busy times – weekends, bank holidays, Christmas Eve and so on.

PARTY-PLAN SELLING

I did this for a while and I must tell you that it is great fun but very hard work. It may be the scheme for you if you have plenty of stamina and want to make serious money; or more correctly, the scheme for you and a dependable friend because this type of selling calls for a partnership and preferably a dynamic duo!

Decide in advance whether you want to show samples at the party and take orders, or take as much stock as possible and sell it there and then.

Taking Samples If you are taking orders from a sample you can, in effect, sell the same thing over and over again on the same night but you must fix realistic delivery times both for yourself, so that you are not constantly working in a panic, and to maintain the customers' interest. You can always adjust delivery dates to give yourself more time when things start getting busy. If you are doing a lot of parties, your stock will tend to get chipped and broken – wine is often served at these parties, you know – but this does not matter as much when you carry samples as you can explain why they look slightly dog-eared.

Selling Stock In this case, the number of parties has to be limited to the amount of stock which you can produce. As you never know beforehand whether the party is going to be mediocre or a raving success, you should limit yourself to the number of parties you could run if they were all sell outs. The inevitable consequence of not limiting party requests is that you are always in a state of panic, wondering if you are going to have enough stock for the next event and on some occasions almost hoping that you will not sell too much.

Selling and Taking Orders The answer is to compromise. Personalised items, like initials, usually have to be ordered and one or two other items also fall into that sort of category, when the customer will want to stamp her own particular mark on a design. Stock items which are known to be good sellers are probably best sold on the night.

Selling Other Modellers' Work You can take work from other dough modellers and add your own mark up. You must keep accurate records and always give them an itemised receipt as well as being prepared to pay for any breakages.

Organising the Party It is a good idea to have your first party at home and ask as many people as you can squeeze in. Then, rather than let people wander around at random for the entire evening, as soon as all the guests have arrived, ask for silence and inflict your sales talk on them.

Your presentation should be short and interesting, describing the dough and how it is made. Give a clear idea of what you are offering in the way of designs and service. Finish by mentioning that you are looking for hostesses to give further parties. Plan to offer a cash incentive based on a percentage of the takings or dough to a similar value.

Set a few rules for yourself and your hostess-to-be to avoid the unhappy occurrence of finding yourself making a presentation to a room full of nothing more inspiring than the hostess and her cat. For example, you might decide that you will not hold a party for less than ten

guests and then only if they fall within an eight mile radius of your home. If the hostess is unfortunate enough to live farther away, then she will have to drum up at least fifteen guests. Telephone the hostess two or three days before the event to check that all the conditions are going to be met and that she has remembered that she is having a party!

CRAFT FAIRS

These are a lot of fun and they can provide a reasonable income if you work hard and are careful about the fairs you attend. There are specialist magazines which publish detailed lists of countrywide fairs throughout the year. Fairs advertised in these magazines are usually run by experienced organisers in a professional way. Answers to the following queries should arrive with the booking form, without any prompting from you; however, if information is sparse do not hesitate to telephone the organiser before booking.

● How much and what type of advertising is planned? Ask about newspapers, posters and local radio.

● You should know the number of stalls and the entrance fee. These are related as customers will not pay a high fee for visiting only a handful of stalls.

● Parking facilities are important to you for unloading and to customers who will not bother to stop if parking is in the least bit troublesome.

● There should be signs and banners directing traffic to the venue.

● Is there electricity available on your stall?

● Will there be other dough modellers at the fair? One more is acceptable, two are excessive.

● What is the fee for exhibitors? It should include the table and use of electricity but sometimes these things are charged separately.

Stall Fees and Deposits These vary widely depending on how prestigious the venue is and the level of advertising planned. If you have all the relevant information you should be able to judge whether you are likely to get value for money. You usually have to pay a deposit when booking in advance. Most professional craftsmen book for the year and normally pay their deposits by the end of January which is advisable as stalls at good fairs are booked very quickly. When you are first starting, paying several deposits in advance can involve quite a large financial outlay but most organisers will accept post-dated cheques and some of them run schemes which lessen the burden provided that you attend several of their fairs throughout the year.

It is sensible to book yourself into several good fairs over a realistic period of time but always leave sufficient time between fairs to replenish your stock.

Designing Your Stall You will have to do something more enterprising than throwing a cloth over your bare table if you want to sell your wares and impress the organiser. Tables at craft fairs are usually of the folding, trestle type and they tend to measure about 1.8 × 0.75m (6 × 2½ft). You cannot rely on this, though, so your display has to be suitable for tables of all sorts of sizes and shapes, as well as being light and capable of folding into nothing in the car. Most people manage to build some kind of display structure from garden trellis which is then fixed to the table using 'G' clamps.

With an attractive cloth, and possibly a canopy over the top, trellis can provide a practical base for hanging dough models. To complete your display you should invest in a couple of clip-on spotlights to highlight your work, and make the paint and varnish sparkle.

TEMPLATES

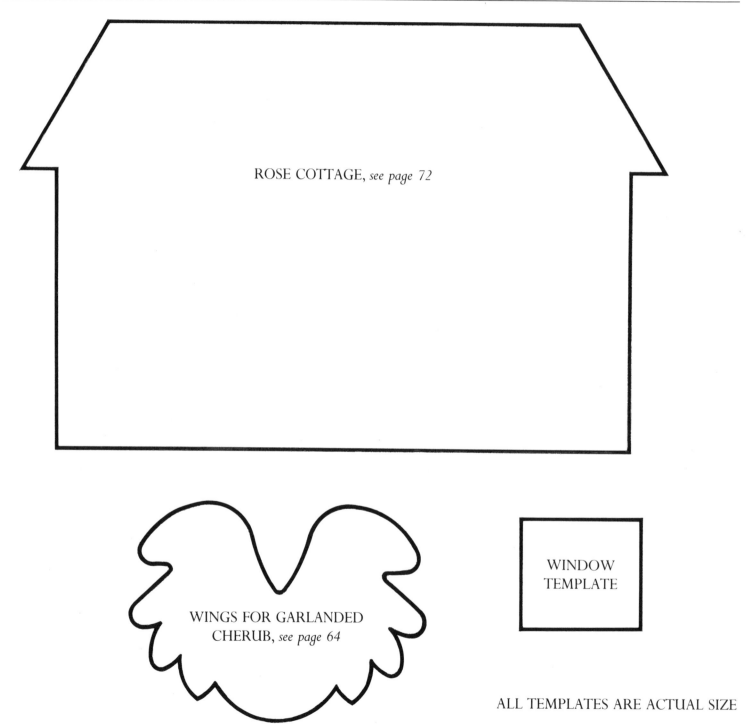

ROSE COTTAGE, *see page 72*

WINGS FOR GARLANDED
CHERUB, *see page 64*

WINDOW
TEMPLATE

ALL TEMPLATES ARE ACTUAL SIZE

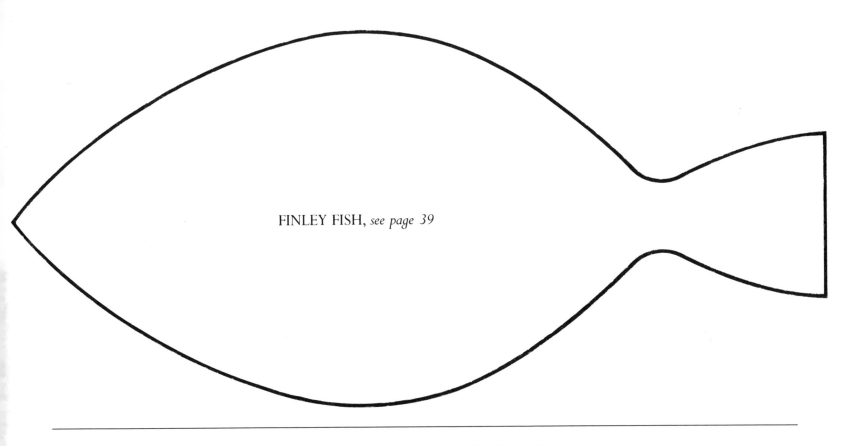

FINLEY FISH, *see page 39*

ACKNOWLEDGEMENTS

The author and publisher would like to thank the following for assistance in the production of this book.

The Art and Stationery Centre,
15, Tolworth Broadway,
Surbiton,
Surrey.

Blackburns Fine Foods,
108, Alexandra Drive,
Surbiton,
Surrey KT5 9AG.

Merehurst is a leading publisher of craft books and has an excellent range of titles to suit all levels. Please send to our address on page 2 for a free catalogue, stating the title of this book.

INDEX